Telephoning in English

B. Jean Naterop and Rod Revell

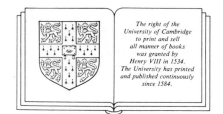

The right of the
University of Cambridge
to print and sell
all manner of books
was granted by
Henry VIII in 1534.
The University has printed
and published continuously
since 1584.

Cambridge University Press

Cambridge

New York   Port Chester

Melbourne   Sydney

Published by the Press Syndicate of the University of Cambridge
The Pitt Building, Trumpington Street, Cambridge CB2 1RP
40 West 20th Street, New York, NY 10011-4211, USA
10 Stamford Road, Oakleigh, Melbourne 3166, Australia

© Cambridge University Press 1987

First published 1987
Sixth printing 1991

Designed by Linda Reed

Printed in Great Britain
at The Bath Press, Avon

ISBN 0 521 26975 X Book
ISBN 0 521 26429 4 Cassette

CONTENTS

ACKNOWLEDGEMENTS

The authors would like to thank York Language Training for assistance from colleagues and friends; Gary Hayes for contributing the US calls; and John Block for help at the initial stage.

The authors and publishers are grateful to the following for permission to reproduce texts and illustrations:
British Telecom for the texts, illustrations and advertisements on pages 16, 25, 48, 68 and 87; Swedish Telecom for the texts and illustrations on pages 37, 58, and 77–8; Jeremy Pembrey for the photographs on pages 7, 17, 27, 39, 49, 59, 69 and 79.

SELF-STUDY GUIDE

For learners using the course without a teacher.

WHO IS TELEPHONING IN ENGLISH FOR?

If you know some English already and would like to learn the sort of English that will help you to answer an English phone call, to make telephone calls in general and for business purposes, then this material is suitable for you. You will learn to *understand* people when they are speaking about normal business matters. Most of the voices you will hear are British and American but you will also hear how people from other parts of the world speak English. You will learn to *speak* in a way that will help you when you need to make and answer business telephone calls. You will also *read* about the many new developments that are happening in the world of telecommunications and about how to get the most out of your telephone.

USING TELEPHONING IN ENGLISH WITHOUT A TEACHER

The material consists of a book and two C60 cassettes. It is divided into eight units. The instructions below tell you what to do in each unit. It is not possible to say how much time you will need for each unit. This will depend on your knowledge of English and the way in which you learn. Work at the speed that is best for you. But remember that it is better to do a little work often than a large amount of work but not very often.

The answers to **Task 11** in each unit are on the cassettes. The answers to the other tasks are in the Key (pages 108–123).

INSTRUCTIONS

Section	Instructions
Listening	1 There are six telephone conversations in this section. Listen to the first two conversations once to get a general idea of what they are about. *Do not read* them in your book. 2 Listen again in more detail. As you listen, do **Task 1**. Again, *do not read* the conversations. 3 Listen again until you understand. Do **Task 2**. Do not look at the text in your book unless it is absolutely necessary. 4 Check the answers to **Task 1** and **2** in the Key. 5 Study 'What to say – what to expect'. Make sure that you understand all the phrases there. 6 Now do **Tasks 3** and **4** and check your answers in the Key. 7 Repeat instructions 1 and 2 above for the second pair of conversations. Do **Task 5** and check your answers. 8 Study the second 'What to say – what to expect' carefully. Make sure you understand it all. 9 Repeat instructions 1, 2 and 3 for the third pair of conversations. Do **Tasks 6** and **7** and check your answers in the Key. 10 Do **Task 8** and check your answers in the Key.
Language study	1 Look at the examples in each of the exercises (**Tasks 9** and **10**) carefully. 2 Write your answers for each of the exercises. 3 Check your answers in the Key.
Speaking	1 Listen to the first Speaking exercise on the cassette (**Task 11**). The voices on the cassette will ask you for information. You will find this in your book under **Task 11**. Say what you think is necessary in the pause. After the pause, the voice on the cassette will give you the correct answer. Repeat the exercise until what you say is the same as what the voice on the cassette says. 2 **Task 12** provides some short situations on cassette where you are required to make the appropriate responses. Say what you think is necessary in the pauses. Suggested responses are given in the Key. You may listen to the cassette first if necessary. Repeat the exercise for further practice. 3 If you can find another learner or English-speaking person, do the role play (**Task 13**). Here you can act out freely what you have learnt in the unit.
Telecom services	1 Read the instructions for **Task 14** carefully. 2 Look at the text and any other information carefully. 3 Try to give the answers asked for. 4 Check your answers in the Key. 5 If your answer is not the same as the one in the Key, look at the task again and try to see why.

This symbol shows you where it is necessary to use the cassettes.

TEACHER'S NOTES

PRELIMINARY

The aim of *Telephoning in English* is to provide up-to-date and relevant practice material for developing skills in comprehending phone calls and making calls for general and business purposes.

It has been designed for people working in business and commerce with a need to improve their active and passive ability when making phone calls in English and for people being trained in vocational, secretarial and management training establishments for a wide variety of jobs in business and commerce. It is envisaged that the material will have broad appeal for employees, actual and future, working at all levels from the secretarial to the junior executive.

The material has an entry point, in traditional terms, at the pre-intermediate level. In terms of the Council of Europe's specifications, the entry point is between Waystage and Threshold.

The primary emphasis is, not surprisingly, on listening and speaking. However, associated writing tasks, such as note and message taking, are practised and there is a minor reading component designed to broaden the learner's knowledge of telephone uses and telecommunication developments.

STRUCTURE AND USE OF THE MATERIAL

Listening

This is the longest section in each of the eight units. It provides the main thematic and linguistic input for the unit. Each section contains six telephone dialogues arranged in three pairs. The middle pair has American voices (except in Unit 1), the first and final pairs have British and non-native voices. The comprehension activities in this section are designed to encourage the extraction of general and detailed information, and to give practice in information recording techniques appropriate to telephone usage.

WHAT TO DO

Introduce the conversations briefly. Play them through once without stopping so that the learners can get a general idea of the contents. Discuss the conversations with them to make sure that there are no major misunderstandings. Play the conversations again so that the learners can do the comprehension tasks while they listen. If there are two comprehension tasks, play the conversations once more. Discuss the learners' answers with them. At this stage, you may like to play the conversations again and allow the learners to read at the same time in order to confirm their understanding. They should, in any case, not have looked at the text of the conversations before this stage. All, except the first pair, are printed at the back of the book (pp 89–104).

Between work on pairs of conversations, you should make sure that the learners have studied and know all the 'What to say – what to expect' items. Doing **Tasks 3, 4** and **8** will also confirm that they can apply what they have learnt.

Language study

A pair of language items that are felt to be appropriate to the type of call being studied and to the learners' level of ability in English are taken out for detailed study and exercise. The approach to these items and the way they are exercised are varied.

Introduce each of the language points covered by the exercises in this section. Discuss any difficulties and provide further examples if necessary. Ask the learners to do the exercises. Provide assistance if necessary. Check the answers orally.

Speaking

There are three activities in this section. The first two (**Tasks 11** and **12**) are recorded on one of the cassettes. **Task 11** is designed to give the learner practice in one of a number of key spoken activities used in business telephone calls. **Task 12** provides situations on tape where the student is required to make appropriate responses in the pauses. Suggested responses are given in the Key. **Task 13** (role play) enables pairs of learners to simulate real calls and apply the language they have learnt in the course of the unit.

In the first Speaking exercise (**Task 11**), introduce the language point that is exercised. Give further examples if necessary. Ask the class to listen to the prompts on the tape and produce appropriate responses before they hear the model responses. This work can be done by the whole class, groups, pairs or individuals. **Task 12** is best done individually. Help to set the scenes and allow students to listen to the cassette first if necessary. Ask students to repeat the exercise for further practice. If you have access to a language laboratory, it could be of use when doing these exercises.

Each unit contains a number of role plays (**Task 13**) that can be done by learners in pairs. In each of the role plays notes are provided for the CALLER (A) and the PERSON WHO ANSWERS (B). The A notes are at the back of the book (pages 105 to 107) while the B notes are included in the units. Each pair of learners can do any or all of the role plays in any order. They may also reverse roles after the first completion of the role play. The role plays should not be attempted until you are reasonably confident that your learners have mastered the relevant language since this activity is an opportunity for free application and expression and is not easily monitored.

Telecom services

Each unit contains a reading passage or activity that suggests ways in which the learners can get the most out of their telephones and presents new services and facilities that are available in the field of telecommunications. The techniques most frequently used in this section are information transfer, problem solving and topic-based reading.

Ask the students to read the text and study any accompanying material so as to get the general meaning. They should then repeat this in order to gain a more detailed understanding. Ask them to do the activity associated with each task and then check the answers with the class as a whole.

OVERVIEW

	Listening	Language study	Speaking	Reading
Unit 1 Who's calling, please?	Identifying people	Requesting information Countries and Nationalities	Spelling Role plays	Making a call
Unit 2 Would you hold on, please?	Connecting people Wrong numbers	Asking questions Note-taking	Giving dates Role plays	Radiopagers
Unit 3 I'd like to know your prices	Inquiries for prices and discounts	Passing on messages Note-taking	Abbreviations / spelling Role plays	International direct dialling
Unit 4 We're ready to order now	Ordering	Talking about the future Nouns and verbs	Giving references and numbers Role plays	Answering machines
Unit 5 I'll have to change the booking	Hotel and travel arrangements	Probability and possibility Reporting questions	Question tags Role plays	Text communication
Unit 6 Let's fix another date	Changing appointments Conferences	Future possibilities Group nouns	Giving information / spelling Role plays	Payphones
Unit 7 What seems to be the trouble?	Making and receiving complaints	Apologising Getting things done	Figures and calculations Role plays	Telephone and TV conferences
Unit 8 I'm sure we can sort it out	Improving the company image	Fault diagnosis Nouns and verbs	Giving information Role plays	Viewdata (Prestel)

1 WHO'S CALLING, PLEASE?

LISTENING

Task 1

Listen to the two telephone conversations on the cassette *before* you read them in your book. While you are listening, complete the table below.

Call	Number called	Country of meeting	Where is called person?
1		*Singapore*	
2	*515 56 24*		

GETTING THROUGH

Sheila Clark:	278 0040.
Georg Wenzel:	Hello, is Harry Bild there?
Sheila Clark:	I'll see if he's in the office. Who's calling?
Georg Wenzel:	Wenzel, Georg Wenzel.
Sheila Clark:	Hold the line, please ... He's in a meeting with the Managing Director at the moment, I'm afraid. Can I help you?
Georg Wenzel:	Well, I met Mr Bild when we were both at the Singapore trade fair. He suggested I should call him when I got back to Europe. When could I reach him?
Sheila Clark:	I don't think the meeting will go on much longer. Shall I ask him to call you when he's free?
Georg Wenzel:	Yes, that would be easiest.
Sheila Clark:	Could I have your name again, please?
Georg Wenzel:	Ah yes, it's Georg Wenzel. W-E-N-Z-E-L.
Sheila Clark:	And the number?
Georg Wenzel:	I'm in Hamburg. From England it's 010 49 40 80 70 55.
Sheila Clark:	Right, you'll be hearing from Mr Bild later in the morning then. Goodbye.
Georg Wenzel:	Thank you for your help. Bye bye.

CALLING BACK LATER

Mary Wilson:	515 56 24. Mary Wilson.
Ahmed Mansour:	Ah, good morning Mrs Wilson. My name is Ahmed Mansour. I'd like to speak to your husband, if I may.
Mary Wilson:	I'm afraid he's not in. He's at a conference in Manchester all day. Can I give him a message?
Ahmed Mansour:	Well, when we met in Saudi Arabia, he asked me to call him when I was in London. I'm flying back tomorrow. Will he be at home this evening?
Mary Wilson:	Yes, he'll be back at about eight thirty.
Ahmed Mansour:	Fine, I'll ring him at about nine then.
Mary Wilson:	Right, I'll tell him you called. Bye bye.
Ahmed Mansour:	Goodbye, Mrs Wilson.

Task 2 🔲

Listen to the calls in Task 1 again. Write a note for each of the absent people.

1

TELEPHONE MESSAGE

Time . . . . Date . . . .

Call from . . . .

to . . . .

Signed . . . .

2

_____ *called.*

_____

_____

_____

_____ *Mary*

What to say – what to expect

You have heard, and will hear again, phrases like these. Read them and make sure you understand them.

ANNOUNCING IDENTITY

Person calling
Hello, this is Sue, Sue James.
Simpson here.
My name is Jack Simpson.
I'm Jack Simpson. Good morning.

Person called
7214.
Simpson here.

ASKING IF SOMEONE IS IN

Person calling
Can I speak to Mr Bild, please?
Hello, is George there by any chance?
Could you put me through to Mrs Dylan, please?
I'd like to speak to your husband if I may.

PERSON WANTED IS NOT THERE

Person called
I'm afraid she isn't in at the moment.
Sorry, she's just gone out. Would you like to ring back later?
He's away for a few days. Can I give him a message?
He's out of town this week, I'm afraid.

WHEN WILL THE PERSON WANTED BE IN?

Person calling
What time could I reach her?
Will he be at home this evening?
Can I contact him on Saturday?
Right, I'll phone again next week.

RINGING OFF

Person calling
Thanks a lot. Goodbye.
I'll get back to you soon.
OK. Bye bye.

Person called
Thanks a lot. Goodbye.
Thanks for calling.
OK. Bye bye.

Task 3

Choose the missing words from the box.

1 Hello, who's that ....?
2 Just a ...., please.
3 I'll .... if she's here.
4 I'll get the information you want; ...., please.
5 You asked me to .... when I was in town again.
6 Sorry, he's not .... at the moment.
7 You can .... him any evening .... six o'clock.
8 Well, I can ring .... later if it's convenient.

after	back	calling	hold the line
in	moment	reach	ring up	see

Task 4

Choose the best answers.

1 I'd like to speak to Mr Kahn, please.
    a Yes.
    b I'm afraid he's not here at the moment.
    c Well, you can't.

2 Can I speak to Mr Kahn, please?
    a Hold on please.
    b Don't go away.
    c All right.

3 Could I speak to Mr Kahn, please?
    a Who's calling?
    b Who are you?
    c What's your name?

4 Who's speaking?
    a I am Fred Bentley.
    b This is Fred Bentley here.
    c Fred Bentley speaking.

5 Can I ring you back later?
    a Yes, ring me.
    b Yes, please do.
    c Of course, yes.

6 When can I reach you?
    a One hour.
    b When you want.
    c I'll be in all evening.

Task 5

Now listen to the following two telephone conversations. Fill in the table as you listen.

Call	Person called	Caller	Request	Who will make the next call?
1				
2				

You will find the tapescript on page 89.

Task 6

Listening check

1 What sort of work does Maria Edwardes do?
2 How is Ron Benson going to find out Maria Edwardes' address?
3 What's the order number?
4 What have IBD Industries ordered from Garston Motors?
5 When would IBD Industries like delivery of their order?

What to say – what to expect

You have heard, and will hear again, phrases like these. Read them and make sure you understand them.

Person calling

I'd like to speak to somebody about...?
Can you help me to find out something about...?
What's the position on...?
Can you deliver them sooner than we agreed?
We'd like earlier delivery if possible.
Could you bring delivery forward by a few weeks?

Person called

What's the order number?
Can you give me the reference number?
When did you place the order?
Well, I'll have to check with the workshop.
I can't tell you right now, but I can look into it.
Can I let you know the situation tomorrow?
I'll ring you back if you like.

Task 7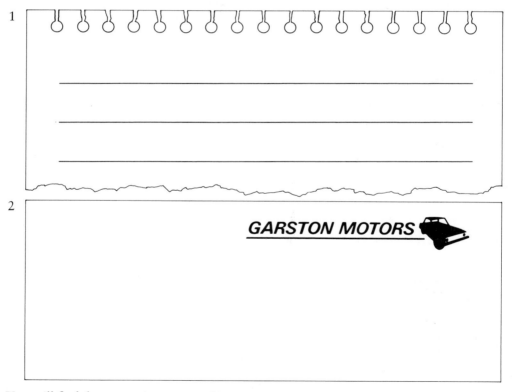

Now listen to Ron Benson and Mr Datta of Garston Motors ringing back as they said they would. Take notes on the two calls on the message pads below.

GARSTON MOTORS

You will find the tapescript on page 90.

Task 8

Complete the following conversations with phrases from the list below. Use each phrase only once.

Hello, is that 10127?
1 ....
Can I speak to Jack Simpson, please?
2 ....
I see. Well, what time will he be there?
3 ....
Right, I'll ring again then. Thanks a lot.
4 ....
Goodbye.

Meg Owen.
5 ....
Oh, I'm fine, thanks. You know, you gave my address to a friend of yours?
6 ....
That's right. Roger O'Hare, that was his name. Do you know what I've done? I can't find his phone number.
7 ....
Ah, thanks very much. I can call him back now. That's a real help.
8 ....
Yes, it would be nice to see you again. Goodbye for now.

9 ....
I'd like to speak to someone about putting forward a delivery.
10 ....
11 ....
I'm phoning about our order for three motors.
12 ....
Yes, it's FC / 172 / Y. We'd like earlier delivery if possible.
13 ....
OK. Could you ring me back today?
14 ....
That'll be fine. Thanks very much.

a   I'll put you through to Order Inquiries.
b   From about two this afternoon.
c   I'll look it up for you. . . . It's 01 420 5071.
d   Yes, late this afternoon if that's convenient.
e   Yes, it is. Can I help you?
f   Not at all. We must meet and have a drink some time.
g   I'm afraid he's out of the office at the moment.
h   Garston Motors. Can I help you?
i   Right. Well, I'll have to check with the workshop.
j   Can you give me the order number?
k   The one who does computer software?
l   Order Inquiries. Can I help you?
m   Oh, hello, Meg. How are you keeping?
n   You're welcome. Goodbye.

LANGUAGE STUDY

Task 9 Requesting information

We can ask for information politely in different ways.

Examples:
You don't know a caller's name.   (*give*)
   Could *you give me your name, please?*
You aren't sure of the name of the caller's company.   (*repeat*)
   Would *you repeat your company's name, please?*
You want to know where the caller is ringing from.   (*tell*)
   Can *you tell me where you're ringing from, please?*

Now make questions using *could*, *would* and *can* in a similar way.

1 You aren't sure who the caller wants to speak to.   (*tell*)
2 You want to know the caller's telephone number.   (*give*)
3 You don't know the spelling of the caller's name.   (*spell*)
4 You didn't hear the caller's address clearly.   (*repeat*)
5 You don't know when the caller will be in the office tomorrow.   (*tell*)
6 You aren't sure about your order's delivery date.   (*confirm*)

Task 10 Countries and nationalities

Fill in the table below with the missing countries and nationalities. Use your dictionary if necessary.

Nationality	Country	Nationality	Country
1	China	Swiss	9 ....
American	2	10	Brazil
Jordanian	3	Malaysian	11 ....
4	France	12	Sweden
German	5	13	Egypt
6	Japan	Belgian	14 ....
7	Spain	15	Mexico
8	The Netherlands	16	Ireland

SPEAKING

Task 11 🔲

Listen to the callers on the cassette. They will ask you how to spell a number of names. The names are given below. Spell the names and then listen to the correct spelling on the cassette.

1 Denham	3 Fulton	5 Knox	7 Pennock	9 Wabsworth
2 Jonsson	4 Garvey	6 Urquhart	8 Joinel	10 Esterhazy

Task 12 🖭

1 You work in an office with Bob, Jean and Chris.
Look at the 'Time out sheet' below, which shows where your colleagues will be during the day. Reply to the calls that come through to your office.
Do the task twice. The first time it is 11.30 a.m. The second time it is 3.00 p.m.

TIME OUT	*Wed 5 August*		
	BOB	JEAN	CHRIS
9-10	May be in late today – have to take.	↑	↑ Visiting Essex Computers Ltd.
10-11	car to garage		should be back ↓ 10.45 ish.
11-12	↑ Sales meeting ↓ PART I	Working at home, no. 85471	↑ Will be in ↓ warehouse.
12-1	LUNCH	↓	
1-2	↑ Sales meeting ↓ PART II	↑ Afternoon off	↑ LUNCH ↓
2-3	If I'm not around I'll have gone home. Can	– do not disturb	↑ Meeting with Pat. ↓
3-4	be contacted there if urgent No. 34298	↓	

2 Now you are making the following calls. Respond to the person who answers your call on the cassette.
a You are ringing Mr Mayo at Essex Electronics.
b You have just phoned this person, who is a close business associate of yours.
c You're phoning Garston Motors to find out the price of their KS pump motors. You don't know which department you need.
d You've just asked to speak to Ms Neil. If she's not in, leave a message for her to call you back. She has the number.

Task 13   Role play

Work with another student when you do this exercise. Agree which of you is Student A and which is Student B. Student B has information on this page. Student A has information on page 105. Sit back-to-back. Student A should now 'ring' Student B. When you have done the calls once, you can change roles.

B1 You are the operator at Supermotors Inc. The person the caller wants to speak to is on holiday. Take the caller's name and any message.

B2 You are Sarah Williams at Supermotors Inc. You think it will be possible to make the change the caller wants. Get the reference number and say you will ring back. Then ring back.

B3 You are an agent for the Philippine Fruit Export Council. The Marketing Manager for the Pineapple Division at the Council headquarters (2336 Roxas Boulevard, Pasay City, Metro Manila, Philippines) is Mr Emilio Ribano.

TELECOM SERVICES

Task 14

The following text is from a telephone directory. Read it and label the drawing below.

Before you start
Be sure of the number you wish to call; check it in your personal list of numbers or in the directory.
For calls where you need to dial a code before the number you want, check the code in your dialling instructions. It helps to write down the complete code and number before you start to dial.

To dial a call
Lift the handset and listen for the dial tone before you make a call. When you dial, using either a dial or a press-button telephone, don't pause too long between digits. When using a dial make sure that you rotate it firmly round

to the stop and let it return by itself. When pressing buttons make sure that each button is depressed in turn to its full extent and be careful to press only one button at a time. Press the buttons at a steady rate.

Answering calls
Answer your telephone promptly, giving your name, the name of your firm or your number. Keep a message pad handy.

When you finish
Replace the handset promptly and firmly on its rest. This stops the charging if you made the call, and if you fail to do this your line may be temporarily disconnected.

2 WOULD YOU HOLD ON, PLEASE?

LISTENING

Task 1 🔲

Listen to the two telephone conversations on the cassette *before* you read them in your book. While you are listening, complete the table below.

Call	Caller's name	Person wanted	Person answering
1			
2			

CONNECTING TO AN EXTENSION

John Shackleton:	Hello, is that the *Journal of Commerce?*
Operator:	Yes, that's right.
John Shackleton:	Look, I've just tried to get hold of Mrs Atkins by dialling her extension direct but there's no reply. She asked me to call this morning.
Operator:	Well, direct dialling normally works but if you'll hold on, I'll try to connect you. Who's calling, please?
John Shackleton:	Oh, Shackleton's my name.
Operator:	Sorry, I didn't catch that. Could you repeat it?
John Shackleton:	It's Shackleton, John Shackleton.
Operator:	Just a moment, please, Mr Shackleton … Mr Shackleton, I can put you through to Mrs Atkins now.
John Shackleton:	Hello, is that Mrs Atkins …

USING A PAGER

Takiro Watanabe:	This is Takiro Watanabe speaking. Could I speak to John Williams, please?
Operator:	Well, er … he's here today but he may not be in his office right now.
Takiro Watanabe:	Er … he did ask me to phone today. Do you think you could find him for me? Has he got a radiopager?
Operator:	Yes, I'll try to get him on the bleeper. Can you hold on?
Takiro Watanabe:	OK, operator, er … if it doesn't take too long.
Operator:	Sorry, caller, what did you say your name was?
Takiro Watanabe:	It's Watanabe, W-A-T-A-N-A-B-E.
John Williams:	Hello, Mr Watanabe. Thanks for calling. So sorry you've been kept waiting. You must be phoning about …

Task 2 🔲

Listen to the calls in Task 1 again. Decide if the following statements about the calls are true (T) or false (F).

1 John Shackleton tried to make a call straight to Mrs Atkins.	T / F
2 The operator sent someone to look for Mr Williams.	T / F
3 The callers in both calls were asked to call.	T / F
4 'Bleeper' is another term for radiopager.	T / F

What to say – what to expect

You have heard, and will hear again, phrases like these. Read them and make sure you understand them.

CONNECTING TO AN EXTENSION

Person calling	*Person called*
Are you sure he isn't there? Have you tried paging him?	I'll see if she's in. Would you hold on, please?

But he asked me to call this morning.
Would you check if he's in another
   office, please?

Yes, hang on for a moment and I'll put
   you through.
Sorry to keep you waiting.
No, sorry, this is the wrong extension.

DIRECT DIALLING

Person called
Yes, I'll put you through to Mr Weston. But if you ring again, you may like to know
that you can dial him direct. It'll save you time. The number's 851 1123.

(If your switchboard has changed over to direct dialling, remember that any call you
receive may be from outside. Telephones connected to many modern switchboards
with direct dialling have two ringing signals. One is for internal calls, the other for
external calls.)

CONFIRMING ARRANGEMENTS

Person calling / Person called
When you've checked things at your end, would you let me know?
You asked me to call back to tell you if it was OK.
Yes, we can go along with these arrangements.
Well, this is how things stand.

WRONG NUMBER

Person calling
Oh, isn't that Preston Builders? So sorry.
Could I check the number? Isn't it 207 3048?
I must have dialled the wrong number.
Sorry to have troubled you.

Task 3

Choose the missing words from the box.

1 Isn't that 191 2005? That's what I ...., I think.
2 No, this is the wrong .... I'll put you on to the switchboard.
3 Sorry to have .... you.
4 He's not in the office at the moment. But I can try to find him on the ....
5 I haven't got the new number. Shall I call .... inquiries?
6 This is how things .... at our end. I'm afraid there's nothing we can do about
   it.
7 I've .... up on the prices you asked about.
8 Now I can .... the arrangements we made.
9 There have been some .... lately, but I think we'll soon solve them.
10 Can we make another .... for next week, then?

appointment	checked	confirm	dialled	directory
extension	problems	radiopager	stand	troubled

Task 4

Choose the best answers.

1 Can you put me through to Miss
  Evans, please?

  a I'll see if she's in her office at the
    moment.
  b I've got the wrong number.
  c I'll check again.

2 Isn't that Seattle then?

  a No, the number has changed.
  b No, you must have the wrong area
    code.
  c Sorry, I may have dialled the wrong
    extension.

3 You asked me to confirm the dates of
  delivery.

  a Yes, that's the best time for them.
  b Yes, let me just get a note pad to write
    them down.
  c Yes, they'll come to England soon.

4 No, this isn't the Metal Case
  Company.

  a So sorry to have troubled you.
  b I'll call again later.
  c Can you connect me with Mr
    Mansour, please?

5 Miss Pearce asked me to call this
  morning.

  a Sorry, your number is the wrong one.
  b Do you know the area code?
  c But there's no person of that name
    here.

6 We can let you know what sizes are
  available.

  a Thank you. I know them.
  b Thanks. I'm glad that's OK now.
  c Thanks. I can order what we need
    then.

Task 5

Listen to the two telephone conversations on the cassette. While you are listening, complete the table below.

Call	Caller's name	Person (and company) wanted	Person (and company) answering	Reason for call
1				—
2				

You will find the tapescript on pages 90–91.

What to say – what to expect

You have heard, and will hear again, phrases like these. Read them and make sure you understand them.

MAKING AND CONFIRMING ARRANGEMENTS

Person calling
This appointment we've been trying to arrange. Well, Thursday would suit us.
These are the details you asked about.
About the delivery times. The earliest date we can manage is May 1st.
Can we get together to talk about this in detail?
I'll pick you up at the entrance to the bus terminal at 8.30.
You wanted to know the final price. Have you got a note pad handy?
The size you suggested is all right after all.

WRONG NUMBER

Person calling
But I found this number in the yellow pages.
Well, this is the number I was asked to ring.
Sorry. I must have got the wrong area code.

Person called
No, this isn't the number you want.
Who did you say you wanted to speak to?
No, I'm not a forwarding company. This is Mrs Thompson speaking.
Sorry, the number's changed.
I think it's 492 3702, but you might check with directory inquiries.
What number are you calling?
You must have the wrong number. Nobody by that name works here.

Task 6 🖭

Listen to the two telephone conversations on the cassette. While you are listening, complete the table below.

Call	Caller's name	Person spoken to	Reason for calling
1			
2			

You will find the tapescript on pages 91–92.

Task 7 📼

Listening check

1 Who is André Max?
2 How many containers are there and what are their contents?
3 Why won't Pat Thompson be travelling to Belgium soon?
4 What does Ms Lester deal with?
5 Why does she want the surfboards soon?

Task 8

Complete the following conversations with phrases from the list below. Use each phrase only once.

1 ....
Good morning. Could I speak to Jane Lewis, please?
2 ....
Lesley Winwood.
3 ....
She said she'd be in all morning.
4 ....
Jane Lewis.
5 ....
Ah yes, Ms Winwood, it's about . . .

Carl Anderson.
6 ....
Lindberg, did you say?
7 ....
There's no one here by that name.
8 ....
Yes, this is 08 46 46 24.
9 ....
That's all right.

Anglo-Swiss Travel, Heidi Richter.
Morning. Could I speak to John Peat?
10 ....
Peat.
11 ....
Oh, hello Steve. How are things?
12 ....
13 ....
Yes, they're the ones we discussed: the 12th and the 19th.
14 ....
Of course. Bye now.

a Yes, that's right.
b Yes, hold the line and I'll put you through to him.
c Good. You'll confirm that to me in writing?

22

d You asked me to call as soon as possible.
e Hold the line, please, and I'll see if she's in.
f Who's calling, please?
g Morning, John. Steve Jones here.
h Oh, isn't there? Could I check the number?
i Fine. You asked me to call back about the Geneva group.
j Could I speak to Mrs Lindberg, please?
k Hello, I can connect you now.
l Reynolds Bicycles, good morning.
m Oh, I'm sorry. I must have dialled the wrong number.
n Yes. Can you confirm the dates now?

LANGUAGE STUDY

Task 9   Asking questions

Examples:
You want to know where the nearest payphone is.
  Where's the nearest payphone?
Find out how she spells her name.
  How do you spell your name?

Now make questions in a similar way.

1 Find out when Mr Drake will be back.
2 You'd like to know why the sales office hasn't called.
3 Find out when he normally arrives at the office.
4 You want to know why the consignment has been delayed.
5 Find out what you dial for directory inquiries.
6 You're interested in knowing where he's phoning from.
7 You need to know when you could reach him.
8 Find out what the number unobtainable tone sounds like.

Task 10   Note-taking (1)

It is often necessary to take notes during phone conversations. You can do this more easily by shortening:
– *words*   leave out vowels (a, e, i, o, u) e.g. send → *snd*, Wednesday → W*dnsdy*
– *sentences* keep in only the 'content' words (nouns, adjectives, adverbs, important verbs) e.g. please call our office back tomorrow → *call office tomorrow*.

Now write the following words and sentences in note form.

1 transport   6 I'll be driving to the exhibition next week.
2 Japan   7 The consignment has been delayed for one month.
3 recommend   8 I'd like to book a room for two nights.
4 person   9 Can you find me a map of the area?
5 speak   10 When the lamp is lit, you can set up a call.

23

SPEAKING

Task 11

Listen to the callers on the cassette. They will ask when certain things happened or will happen. Tell them, using the dates given below. Then listen to the correct way to say them.

1 4 March 1981   5 Thursday 2 July
2 Wednesday 12 April   6 29 August 1983
3 7 May 1985   7 13 June
4 Tuesday 21 April   8 31 December

Task 12 [cassette icon]

You are making the following calls. Respond to the person on the cassette.

1 You are phoning Preston Builders Ltd.
2 You are phoning Kenny Fung at Far Eastern Travel to check on some flight bookings. He asked you to phone him back today.
3 You are ringing Ben Seldeen to confirm an appointment you've been trying to arrange. You suggest Monday.
4 You work in Sales Accounts. You have just picked up your phone.

Task 13 Role play

Work with another student when you do this exercise. Agree which of you is Student A and which is Student B. Student B has information on this page, Student A on page 105. Sit back-to-back. Student A should now 'ring' Student B. When you have made the calls once, you can change roles.

B1 You don't know the person the caller wants to speak to. Has he got the right number? Your number is 75 40 25.

B2 You are Peter Chan. Your wife is away on business in Tokyo for three days. Find out what the caller wants. You think the arrangement is OK but tell the caller that you will get your wife to ring him when she gets back.

B3 You are Bruno Lampard. You are busy all next week except on Thursday from 11.45 a.m.

TELECOM SERVICES

Task 14

This is a newspaper advertisement that appeared recently for British Telecom radio-pagers. Read it and answer the questions below.

When you're out of the office and a new business prospect calls, who's going to tell you? Your secretary? Your sales manager? Your regional manager?

It could be any one of them, and whoever it is you'll need to talk to them fast if you're going to get the business before anyone else.

Carry a British Telecom Radiopager and that's no problem.

Because all our Radiopagers have several different, easily distinguishable tone alerts. So when your sales manager calls, you won't waste time calling your secretary.

Wherever you are, you'll get back to the right person first time, and get to where the latest opportunity is before anyone else.

Only British Telecom Radiopaging offers a service that covers virtually the whole of the UK, at prices you'll find very reasonable. And the service is as flexible as your needs, whether you want to operate

nationally, regionally, or purely locally.

So, wherever business takes you, make sure you know who's calling, with a British Telecom Radiopager.

To find out in detail how British Telecom Radiopaging can help you make the most of every business opportunity, dial 100 and ask for "Freefone Radiopaging," or fill in the coupon.

▶ EFFICIENCY AT WORK

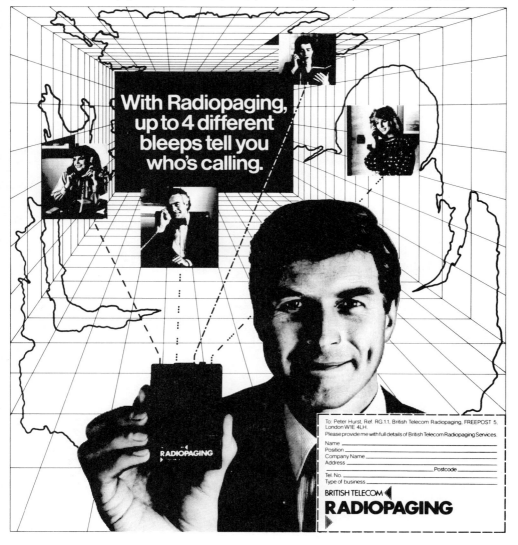

1 What is the maximum number of different tone alerts you can have with one of these radiopagers?
2 Does only British Telecom offer radiopaging in Britain?
3 Is it possible to have a radiopager that operates in only one area?
4 How much does it cost to find out about radiopaging?

3 I'D LIKE TO KNOW YOUR PRICES

LISTENING

Task 1 📼

Listen to the two telephone conversations on the cassette. While you are listening, complete the table below.

Call	Caller	Called person / company	Caller interested in
1			
2			

CALLING THE BANK MANAGER

Bank manager:	Parker speaking. Good morning.
Mr Murray:	Good morning. Mr Murray here. You know we were talking about those shares I wanted to get.
Bank manager:	Oh yes, Electroworks it was, I think. It's not a bad time to buy, you know. Prices on the stock market are slack at the moment. But would you excuse me? I'm just talking to a client. Can I ring you back in half an hour? That'll give me time to contact our stocks department for you.
Mr Murray:	Yes, that'll be fine. And at the same time you might let me have a quote on a few industrials too, please. I've been told they're quite favourable now . . .

ASKING ABOUT FLIGHT PRICES

Travel agency:	Globe Travel here. Can I help you?
Customer:	Yes, please. This is Fusako Matsumoto speaking. I'm planning to fly to Penang next month. What's the price of a flight at the moment?
Travel agency:	Well, er, that depends. D'you want to fly first or economy class? When will you be going? And how long would you like to stay?
Customer:	Well, I'm planning a short holiday, maybe ten days or so. But I don't want a package tour. Just the flight, er, economy class I suppose.
Travel agency:	And when is it you'd like to leave?
Customer:	On Friday the 9th June.
Travel agency:	Then I can get you an excursion ticket. That's on Malaysian Airlines and it'll cost HK$1950 return.
Customer:	And what would it be if I flew Cathay Pacific?
Travel agency:	Now, let's see. That's ten days' time. It's only slightly more, HK$2160 in fact.
Customer:	Well, I'll have to think about . . .
Travel agency:	There is one thing with the Cathay Pacific flight. The time might be more convenient for you because it leaves rather later in the morning, at 11.40. That's CP 432.
Customer:	And the other one? When's that?
Travel agency:	That's much earlier, at 9.40. That means you're in Penang at about 12 noon, whereas the Cathay Pacific flight lands at about half past two.
Customer:	Er . . . I'll have to think about that. Er, what about the return flight? Could you tell me . . .

Task 2 🔲

Listen to the calls in Task 1 again. Take notes on the note pads.

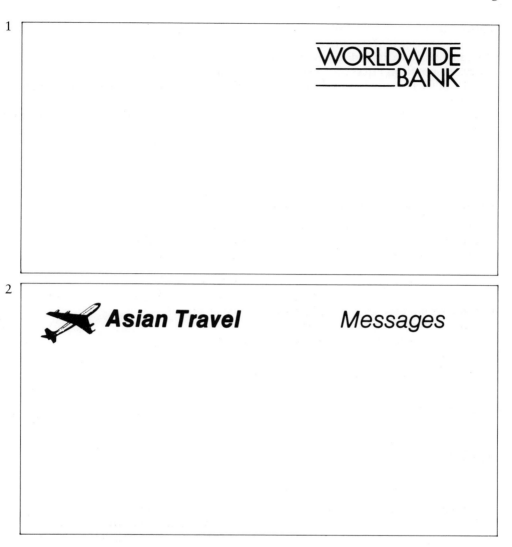

1
WORLDWIDE BANK

2
Asian Travel   *Messages*

What to say — what to expect

INQUIRIES FOR PRICES AND DISCOUNTS

Person calling
I've seen your advertisement in the *Builder's Journal* and I'd like to know your prices and terms.
What's the price of the Portland cement you're offering?
If your terms are reasonable, we'll be able to place another order soon.
Could you let us have a firm offer?
We sell pumps and need regular supplies.
What are your hotel rates? Does that include breakfast and other extras?

Person called
Our lowest price is $60 a dozen.
We can give you a 10% discount if your order reaches us by October 30th.
Sorry, it's not firm. Prices are likely to go up soon.
No, I can't tell you what the discount is until I know how many you'd like to order.
 You see, it depends on the quantity.
Yes, if your order's over $10 000 in value, we can go along with the special discount
 terms.

Task 3

Choose the missing words from the box.

1 These are our .... prices for the material you wanted.
2 Couldn't you manage to .... me a better discount for this large ....?
3 That's not much more than the price you paid last year. They've only ....
 a little.
4 There's a very heavy .... for our tents this year.
5 We can offer you a .... discount if you order before the end of the month.
6 What would they .... if I took a hundred at a time?
7 Yes, but don't forget that this is a .... order.
8 .... prices are quoted on the stock market.

allow	cost	demand	gone up	lowest
quantity	repeat	share	special	

Task 4

Choose the best answers/explanations.

1 Can you give me a quotation?
  a We haven't any more available.
  b This price is very competitive.
  c They cost $3.30 each.

2 You wanted a higher discount.
  a It depends on the number you order.
  b The prices are our lowest.
  c It's not so much.

3 We are thinking of buying your
 products.
  a Then take advantage of our
   introductory offer.
  b Business is good at present.
  c Share prices have been falling lately.

4 Can you offer the large size at the
 same price?
  a No, it's cheaper.
  b No, it's more expensive.
  c No, the price is unchanged.

5 The terms are CIF.	a No credit is allowed.
	b Goods are supplied only if cash is firm.
	c Goods are sent to the customer's place.
6 Are those your most favourable prices?	a Yes, we have plenty available.
	b Yes, we can't reduce them.
	c Yes, they are very important.

Task 5

Listen to the two telephone conversations on the cassette. While you are listening, take notes on the note pads.

1

NOTES
_____

2

From the desk of Sam Rizzo

You will find the tapescript on page 92.

What to say – what to expect

INQUIRIES FOR PRICES AND DISCOUNTS

Person calling

This is a special introductory offer. We'd like a lot of new customers to try our drinks.

Is this February price list still valid?

We usually get a better discount on a repeat order.

Is that your best quote? I thought prices would be coming down now.

Are you still running that late summer special on office equipment?

Person called

Those are the best terms we can offer, I'm afraid, Don.

Have you checked with our competitors? You'll find our prices can't be beaten.

The quotation is CIF Venezuela so the prices include freight and insurance.

It would take too long to give you all the prices and terms on the phone. Why don't I send you our price list by special delivery? You'll have it by tomorrow.

Task 6 📼

Listen to the two telephone conversations on the cassette. While you are listening, fill in the table below.

Call	Caller	Company called	Type of article asked about	Ref no.	Price	Discount
1	a	b	c	d e	f g	
2	a	b	c		d	e

You will find the tapescript on pages 92–93.

Task 7 📼

Listening check

1 On what quantity does Mr Gilbert base his prices?
2 What will Mr Gilbert send Pat Thompson?
3 What quality are the footballs?
4 What is the 9% discount made up of?
5 How will Mr Hampton make out his order?

Task 8

Complete the following conversation with phrases from the list below. Use each phrase only once.

Carstairs Ltd.
Could I speak to Mr Cooper, please? Ray Cooper.
1 ....
Oh, that's a pity.
2 ....
Yes, I'd like to place an order for some printers.
3 ....
Hello, is that Mr Winchester?
4 ....
I'm ringing from Computer Sales Ltd. We'd like to order some A42 printers.
5 ....
6 ....
Oh yes, until the end of the year.
7 ....
You've done business with us before, haven't you?
Yes, and this is our second order for this type of printer.
8 ....
9 ....
Oh, we don't normally go over 10%.
10 ....
I see. Well, I'd better confirm that with him.
11 ....
Yes, Computer Sales Ltd, you said. And your name is...?
Fowles, Trevor Fowles.
12 ....

a I see. How many would you like?
b We're thinking in terms of $12\frac{1}{2}\%$.
c Yes, do that and then perhaps you'll call me back.
d I'll put you through to Mr Winchester, then.
e I'm afraid he's not in yet.
f Right, Mr Fowles. You'll be hearing from us later in the morning.
g Yes, but we had $7\frac{1}{2}\%$ last time and Mr Cooper said it would be 5% higher for a repeat order.
h What discount would you offer on an order for 100?
i Speaking.
j That's good. We give a better discount on a repeat order.
k Well, it depends on your terms. Is your May price list still valid?
l Is it about an order?

LANGUAGE STUDY

Task 9   Passing on messages

Study these examples of how to pass on messages:
'Tell him we'**ll** offer them a bigger discount,' said the Sales Manager.
  The Sales Manager said that we'd offer you a bigger discount.
'Would you inform Mr Benson that the suppliers **need** confirmation in writing,' said Mr Clark.
  *Mr Clark said that the suppliers **need** confirmation in writing, Mr Benson.*

Pass on the following messages in a similar way using the past or present tense. Make sure that you make all the necessary changes.

1 'Could you tell him I'm arriving on BA 651,' said Sven Larsson.
2 'Tell him I want at least thirty in the first delivery,' said Mr Dutronc.
3 'Let her know she can fly on MAS 1832,' said the travel agency clerk.
4 'Tell him there's an extra 2% discount for cash,' said Peter Novak.
5 'Let Mrs Pertile know I've received her order,' said the Sales Manager.
6 'Tell Mr Blanchard that's the best price we can offer,' said Mr Jackson.
7 'Could you tell Mr Klein that his order has been dispatched,' said the clerk.
8 'Tell my husband I'll wait for him at the restaurant,' said Mrs Reid.

Task 10   Note-taking (2)

Decide which abbreviation matches each of these words and phrases. Abbreviations marked * are mostly found in telexes but they are also useful in note-taking.

1 note	9 as soon as possible
2 for example	10 cost, insurance, freight
3 per year	11 free on board
4 and so on	12 about
5 estimated time of arrival	13 maximum
6 Greenwich Mean Time	14 departure
7 telex	15 for the attention of
8 stamped addressed envelope	16 especially

etc.	ETA	SAE	NB	TLX*	p.a.	CIF	
ASAP*	esp.	RE*	e.g.	max.	dep.	GMT	
ATTN*	fob						

Now use abbreviations to help you shorten the following sentences into notes.

17 Could you ask Mr Dittmar about the invoice as soon as you can?
18 The cost will be $27 000 including insurance and freight.
19 And there'll be interest payable at 18 per cent per year.
20 Their agent is expected to arrive in London at 22.30.
21 It is very important that you observe the changed departure time.

SPEAKING

Task 11 🔲

Listen to the callers on the cassette and answer their questions using the information given below.

1 Burckhardt
2 ETA 10.25 a.m.
3 Farquharson
4 Pysanczyn
5 midday on 27.11.86

6 Gomersall
7 15.30 GMT
8 Jowsey
9 ASAP
10 Velasquez

Task 12 🔲

You have received this letter from a friend in Madrid.

> Calle Columbia 14
>
> Hi!
>   Why don't you come over for a week's holiday? Flights to Madrid are very reasonable. Find out if you can get an excursion ticket around 6th April, then you can spend Easter with us.

Now ring up the travel agent and get some information about flights You don't want to pay more than £165. You may listen to the cassette first to help you.

Task 13   Role play

Sit back-to-back in pairs. Student A, who has information on page 105, should 'ring' student B who has information on this page. Change roles when you have done the calls once.

B1 You are Donald Scott, a salesman with Supersit Inc. Your price per chair (model A1) is $32.95. Discounts for large orders are 7% (up to 500), 10% (up to 1000) and 12% (over 1000). You can, if you wish, increase these by up to 2% but not more. You have a new, better chair (model A2) which costs $40 but there is a special introductory discount of 15% (up to 500) and 20% (above 500).

B2 You work for Global Travel. There are flights from London to Torino at 9.30 (arr. 11.40, British Airways, BA 552, £165 PEX) and at 12.00 (arr. 14.15, Alitalia, AL 791, £145 special price).

B3 You are Jane Lever. You want to buy a Datapower 512 computer. You have seen them at £1100–£1250 in computer shops. You have asked Compsell, a big London computer distributor, to ring and give you a price.

TELECOM SERVICES

Task 14   International direct dialling (IDD)

The map and the instructions are from a brochure written by Swedish Telecom to help foreigners making international calls from Sweden. Look at them carefully and answer the questions below.

1 How many digits do you usually dial before waiting for a tone?
2 What does an eight-minute call to Luxembourg cost, in Swedish crowns?
3 The 'Talking Timetable', a 24-hour recorded message service for York to London trains has the number 34561. The York area code is 0904. How would you ring it from Sweden?
4 What does a six-minute Monday lunchtime call to Canada cost?
5 You normally miss out the first digit of the area code. Name the countries for which you do not miss out this digit.
6 How many countries have three-digit country codes?

Dial your own calls to other countries.

Now you can phone to practically all countries all over the world. 135 countries altogether, but to certain countries you can only dial the call to certain parts or large cities.

In the table below you will find most of what you need to know to be able to dial the number yourself. Here is an example: the weather forecast service in Hamburg:

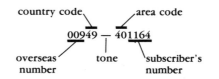

country code   area code

00949 — 401164

overseas   tone   subscriber's
number   number

Dial 00949, wait for a tone, then dial 401164 in sequence. N.B. To most countries you skip the first digit of the area code if it is 0, 8 or 9. Remember the difference in time.

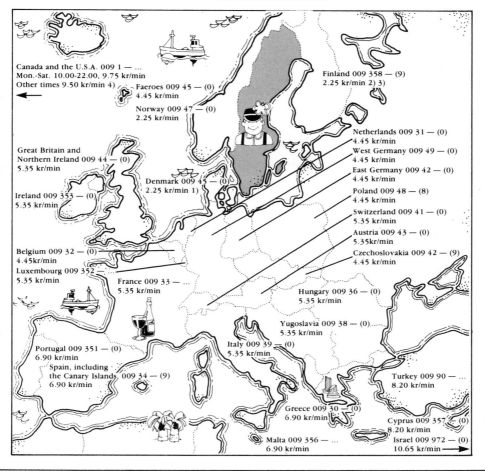

Canada and the U.S.A. 009 1 — ...
Mon.-Sat. 10.00-22.00, 9.75 kr/min
Other times 9.50 kr/min 4)

Faeroes 009 45 — (0)
4.45 kr/min

Norway 009 47 — (0)
2.25 kr/min

Finland 009 358 — (9)
2.25 kr/min 2) 3)

Netherlands 009 31 — (0)
4.45 kr/min

West Germany 009 49 — (0)
4.45 kr/min

East Germany 009 42 — (0)
4.45 kr/min

Great Britain and
Northern Ireland 009 44 — (0)
5.35 kr/min

Denmark 009 45 — (0)
2.25 kr/min 1)

Poland 009 48 — (8)
4.45 kr/min

Switzerland 009 41 — (0)
5.35 kr/min

Ireland 009 353 — (0)
5.35 kr/min

Austria 009 43 — (0)
5.35kr/min

Czechoslovakia 009 42 — (9)
4.45 kr/min

Belgium 009 32 — (0)
4.45kr/min

Luxembourg 009 352 —
5.35 kr/min

France 009 33 — ...
5.35 kr/min

Hungary 009 36 — (0)
5.35 kr/min

Yugoslavia 009 38 — (0)
5.35 kr/min

Portugal 009 351 — (0)
6.90 kr/min

Spain, including
the Canary Islands, 009 34 — (9)
6.90 kr/min

Italy 009 39 — (0)
5.35 kr/min

Turkey 009 90 — ...
8.20 kr/min

Greece 009 30 — (0)
6.90 kr/min

Cyprus 009 357 — (0)
8.20 kr/min

Malta 009 356 — ...
6.90 kr/min

Israel 009 972 — (0)
10.65 kr/min

4 WE'RE READY TO ORDER NOW

LISTENING

Task 1

Listen to the three telephone calls on the cassette. While you are listening, complete the table below.

Call	Company called	Caller	Reason for calling
1			
2			
3		———	

ORDERING A TAXI

Taxi service:	Fast Taxi Service here. Can I help you?
Ms Lee:	Ah yes, please. I'd like a taxi in about ten minutes' time.
Taxi service:	OK. Where are you calling from?
Ms Lee:	I'm at the Singapore Rubber House, Collyer Quay. My name is Lee, Barbara Lee.
Taxi service:	Right. Could you just wait in the entrance hall, please.
Ms Lee:	All right. I'll be there. Let's see . . . that'll be at ten to eleven.
Taxi service:	Yes, OK, ten to eleven. I'll be there. Er . . . where are you going to?
Ms Lee:	I want to go to Changi Airport. I'm catching a plane to Bangkok at 11.25.
Taxi service:	That's OK. I'll be right over.
Ms Lee:	Thanks. Goodbye.

ORDERING FROM A MAIL ORDER CATALOGUE

Customer:	Hello, is that the Reliance Company?
Clerk:	Yes, that's right. Can I help you?
Customer:	Yes, I'd like to place an order for a bicycle I've seen in your catalogue. With a 22-inch frame.
Clerk:	Bicycle? Well, we have three different models. Could you quote the reference number please?
Customer:	I'll just have a look. Here it is – number AD 47301.
Clerk:	Right, I'll just key that in. That's the sports model at £237.50.
Customer:	No, wait a moment, I thought it was £182. Has the price gone up?
Clerk:	If you check, sir, you'll see that the touring model is £182 and the sports one £237.50.
Customer:	You're quite right. It's the sports model I want.
Clerk:	I'll take that order down then, sir. Could I have your name and address? Or do you have an account number?
Customer:	Well, I might have, but I can't tell you what the number is right now.
Clerk:	We can look it up at this end. It doesn't matter. Would you give me your name and address, then?
Customer:	Yes, it's Edward Bronson of 16 Fryent Road, London NW9 4AH.
Clerk:	Sorry, I didn't catch the name of the street. Could you repeat it?
Customer:	Yes, it's 16 Fryent Road. I'll spell it: F-R-Y-E-N-T.
Clerk:	So it's for Mr Edward Bronson, 16 Fryent Road, London NW9 4AH. And how would you like to pay, sir? By cheque or by credit card?
Customer:	I'll pay by cheque, as usual. When can I expect it?
Clerk:	It should reach you within 28 days. Let us know if it doesn't. We'll enclose the bill with the bicycle.
Customer:	That's OK. Thank you. Goodbye.
Clerk:	Thank you for calling, Mr Bronson. Goodbye.

24-HOUR ORDER RECORDING SYSTEM

This is 01 431 9200, City Trading Ltd. There is no one on the premises at the moment, but you can give us your order when you hear the tone. First we shall ask you to give us your name and address, as well as your account number. Then please quote the item number from our catalogue, the quantity of goods requested and the size, where applicable. You'll receive an order acknowledgement from us by mail and we

will dispatch the articles you've ordered as soon as possible. Thank you for calling.
... (TONE) ...

Task 2

Decide if the following sentences are true (T) or false (F).

1 Ms Lee will wait for the taxi on the ground floor   T / F
2 She wants to catch a train to Bangkok.   T / F
3 The customer made a mistake about the price.   T / F
4 Mr Bronson definitely has an account with Reliance.   T / F
5 He normally uses his credit card when he pays.   T / F
6 You must always give the size when you order something from City Trading Ltd.   T / F

What to say – what to expect

ORDERING

Person calling
That offer you sent us was fine. We're
   ready to order now.
We'd like to place an order for 20 dozen.
Can you supply us with the equipment
   from stock?
I'm phoning you with a repeat order.
   Have you got the details of our last
   one?

Person called
As this is a repeat order, we could allow
   you a longer credit period.

DELIVERY

Person calling
We do need the goods urgently. Can you
   dispatch them at once?

Person called
We'll dispatch them immediately from
   stock.
Sorry, there's a three week delivery time.
We'll be able to send your consignment
   before the end of the month.
How would you like delivery to be
   made: by rail, road transport or air
   freight?
The consignment was collected this
   morning. It should reach you by
   Thursday.

AVOIDING MISUNDERSTANDINGS

Person calling / Person called
Sorry, I couldn't hear what you said. Would you mind repeating the price?
I didn't catch what you said. Would you please repeat that last remark?
Could you possibly speak more slowly?
This is a very bad line, I'm afraid. Can I ring you back?

Task 3

Choose the missing words from the box.

1 We've checked your quotation and we'd like to .... an order now.
2 Yes, I'd be pleased to make a .... of it.
3 Can you .... the item number from the ...., please?
4 There's rather a .... We need them urgently.
5 Are you planning to .... by cheque, or do you have a monthly ....?
6 Yes, we'll enclose the .... with the goods.
7 We've got it in stock, so I can .... it immediately.
8 If you like, we can send them by air ....
9 No, it's not our first one. It's a .... order.
10 Sorry, I didn't quite .... what you said. Could you repeat the price?

account	bill	catalogue	catch	dispatch
freight	note	quote	pay	place	repeat	rush

Task 4

Choose the best answers.

1 Where are you calling from?
   a I'm on the phone.
   b My address is 49 Northwick Street.
   c This is Mrs Skolnick speaking.

2 Can't you reduce the price for our first order?
   a There are fewer goods available.
   b The order is firm.
   c It may be possible for an initial order.

3 Why is there no one on the premises right now?
   a The building is quite new.
   b It is after office hours.
   c The person wanted is on holiday.

4 Would you quote the item number, please?
   a Yes, I have your quote.
   b Yes, that's the quantity I want.
   c Yes, I have your price list.

5 Would you prefer the latter?
   a Yes, I'd rather pay later.
   b Yes, I like the suggestion you made in your letter.
   c Yes, the last suggestion is the best one.

6 We've got some more on order.
   a So you expect them to come in soon?
   b So you can't order enough?
   c So you'll have to order some more?

Task 5 🔲

Listen to the two telephone conversations on the cassette. While you are listening, complete the table below.

Call	Company called	Caller's name	Address / location	Order	Time of delivery
1					
2					

You will find the tapescript on page 94.

What to say – what to expect

TRAVEL ARRANGEMENTS

Person calling
Is there a connecting flight to Buffalo out of Kennedy International? (US)
What kind of transportation is available from the airport into town?
Will I have enough time to get into the airport between flights?

Person called
Are you willing to travel stand-by if I can't get you a confirmed seat?
Be sure to call and confirm your international flight at least 48 hours before departure.
You'll have a 12-hour layover in Chicago. (US)

HOTELS

Person calling
I'd like to know the price for a single room with shower for one night, please.
I'd like to make a reservation for Friday 27 August, please.
Are conference room facilities available at your hotel?

Person called
We're fully booked for the night, sir. If you like, we could recommend another hotel.

Task 6 📼

Listen to the next two telephone conversations on the cassette. While you are listening, take a note of the orders on the message pads below.

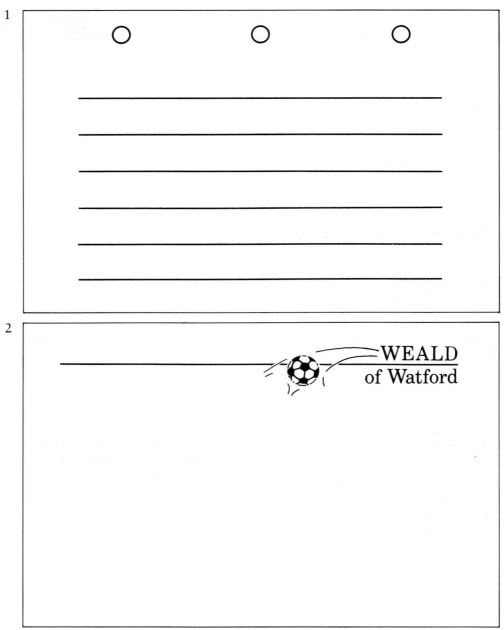

You will find the tapescript on page 95.

Task 7 🔲

Listening check

1 What price reduction will Mr Thompson get for the quantity of tents he wants?
2 How can payment be made?
3 Why do McPhersons need new supplies so soon?
4 Why can't they get the same ones they had before?
5 When will the 'Tournament' shoes be available?

Task 8

Complete the following conversation with phrases from the list below. Use each phrase only once.

London Insurance Ltd. Can I help you?
1 ....
2 ....
Thanks very much.
3 ....
Travel Department.
4 ....
I see. Could you tell me how long you'll be away?
5 ....
Right. Will you be outside Europe at all?
6 ....
Well, we have 10, 20 and 30 day policies so you'll need a 20 day one.
Is it not possible to get cover just for two weeks?
7 ....
Well, it'll have to be 20 days then. How much will it cost?
8 ....
Is there an alternative?
9 ....
But it's better value if I take the full package, I suppose.
10 ....
OK, I'll do that then. What do you need to know?
11 ....

a No, only in France and Germany.
b I'll put you through to our Travel Department.
c Good morning. I'd like some insurance for a journey abroad.
d Well, perhaps we could start with your name and address . . .
e I'm afraid not. We only have standard periods.
f Yes, I'd like some travel insurance.
g Hold the line, please.
h Yes, that's right. And it's simpler, too.
i For full cover – that's death, injury, delay, baggage and money – £17.50.
j For a fortnight, from 19 September.
k Well, you could insure each or any of these categories separately.

LANGUAGE STUDY

Task 9   Talking about the future

Notice how we use the simple present when we talk about a fixed timetable:
> *The next train to Kyoto **leaves** at 10.22.*

and the present continuous when we talk about future arrangements:
> *I'**m meeting** her this evening.*

In the following sentences, put the verb in brackets in the correct form.

1 Tomorrow's Rio flight .... at noon   (*arrive*)
2 We .... some relatives next week.   (*visit*)
3 The bank .... at 10 a.m. tomorrow.   (*open*)
4 The concert .... an hour earlier than usual tonight.   (*start*)
5 They .... to Rome this summer.   (*go*)
6 We .... for lunch at the Grand Hotel tomorrow.   (*meet*)

Task 10   Nouns and verbs

Complete the following table.

Noun	Verb	Noun	Verb
1	deliver	9	reserve
2	inform	10 booking	....
3 cost	....	11 cancellation	....
4	inquire	12 quotation / quote	....
5 charge	....	13	arrange
6	confirm	14 translation	....
7 call	....	15 pager	....
8 suggestion	....	16	fly

SPEAKING

Task 11   🔲

Listen to the callers on the tape. They will ask you for some reference and phone numbers. These are given below.

1 0019   6 A–793 / NCF
2 CIB7 / 79   7 010 254 2 347689
3 ISBN 1 90 374641 9   8 A 43.17
4 S–116 69   9 AA 7342 / X
5 009 44 904 42429   10 1 34 0680

Task 12

Here is an extract from a mail order catalogue. You phone the company to order the goods. You may listen to the cassette first to help you.

XD4986
Lightweight ridge tent
Centre height 1m
Polyester/viscose **£35.00**

Task 13   *Role play*

Sit back-to-back in pairs. Student A, who has information on page 106, should 'ring' student B, who has information on this page. Change roles when you have done the calls once.

B1 You work at the Grand Palace Restaurant. The restaurant is fully booked today between 7 and 10 p.m. If you cannot help the caller, recommend the Minerva Restaurant. It belongs to the same restaurant group and has approximately the same standard and prices. Its phone number is 791 8181 and the address is 17 York Street.

B2 You work at the Minerva Restaurant. Accept the caller's reservation, get his/her name and make sure they know where the restaurant is.

B3 You work at the Sola Beach Hotel, Bergen, Norway. Your room rates are NOK (Norwegian Crowns) 1050 single and 1375 double, including breakfast. The hotel is not full in mid-January.

TELECOM SERVICES

Task 14

Look at the picture of the Robin answering and recording machine on page 48 and read about its controls. Then answer the questions below.

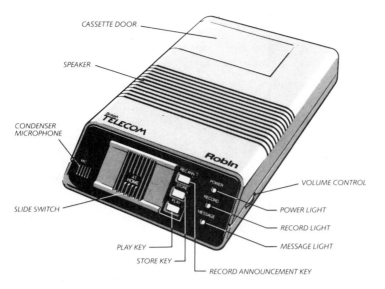

CASSETTE DOOR

SPEAKER

CONDENSER
MICROPHONE

SLIDE SWITCH

PLAY KEY

STORE KEY

RECORD ANNOUNCEMENT KEY

VOLUME CONTROL

POWER LIGHT

RECORD LIGHT

MESSAGE LIGHT

3. The Controls

Most of Robin's functions are totally automatic. Three computerised one-touch keys and a slide switch allow you to operate Robin with ease. The controls are clearly labelled, and their use is fully explained in later sections of this guide. However, here is a brief outline of what each one does.

'REC ANN'– Short for 'Record Announcement'. This key is used for recording the outgoing announcement you want Robin to give to your callers.

'STORE'– This key is used to store any incoming messages you have already listened to once, but wish to hear again later.

'PLAY'– This key plays back to you messages left by your callers.

'THE SLIDE SWITCH'– This has two positions – 'AT HOME', used when you want to answer the telephone personally, or when you wish to use Robin's other controls, and 'ANSWER', used when you want Robin to answer the telephone and record callers' messages.

1 How many controls are there on the front of the machine?
2 Are there any other controls?
3 What do you do if you want to hear incoming messages more than once?
4 What do you do before leaving?

5 I'LL HAVE TO CHANGE THE BOOKING

LISTENING

Task 1 [cassette icon]

Listen to the two telephone conversations on the cassette. While you are listening, complete the table below.

Call	Name of travel agency	Country of destination	Alternatives discussed
1			a b
2			a b

INQUIRING ABOUT A PACKAGE HOLIDAY

Aston:	Aston Tours and Travel. Could you hold on a minute? I'll be with you right away . . .
	Sorry to have kept you waiting. I was on the other line. How can I help you?
Client:	That was a damn long minute. I haven't got all the time in the world, you know.
Aston:	So sorry, sir. But what can I do for you?
Client:	Well, I've got your catalogue, and I think I'd like to go to Spain this Christmas, to the Costa del Sol.
Aston:	The Costa del Sol? Well, we can certainly arrange a wonderful holiday for you there, especially as you're booking quite early. Is it for one person, sir, or more?
Client:	It's for three, actually. My wife and me, and our son.
Aston:	So you'd like a double room and a single. Could I have your name and address, please?
Client:	Hang on just a minute. Your catalogue says there are self-catering apartments, too.
Aston:	That's right. Have you found anything that appeals to you?
Client:	Well, my wife likes the description of those apartments at Marbella, I think it is.
Aston:	A very good choice, if I may say so.
Client:	But I think they're rather a long way from the centre, the golf courses and so on.
Aston:	That's true, but there's a wonderful beach at Marbella, and transport facilities are good in the area.
Client:	What about the holiday bungalows at Torremolinos? They're on the next page . . .

SUPPLYING TRAVEL INFORMATION

Mrs Matsumoto:	Fusako Matsumoto.
Agency:	Good morning, Mrs Matsumoto. Globe Travel on the line. You rang us up a few days ago about a trip you were planning to Penang. Have you made a booking yet?
Mrs Matsumoto:	No, um . . . I haven't done anything yet. I was just planning to phone you in fact.
Agency:	That's a coincidence. Let's see now – you were inquiring about Cathay Pacific flights and Malaysian Airlines, weren't you?
Mrs Matsumoto:	Yes, the Malaysian Airlines flight was a bit more reasonable, wasn't it?
Agency:	That's right, Mrs Matsumoto, but I seem to remember that the time of the other flight was rather more convenient.
Mrs Matsumoto:	Oh, but that doesn't really matter so much in my case. My flat is near the airport. When does the Malaysian Airlines' flight take off, did you say?
Agency:	MAS 174 leaves at 9.40, so check-in's at about half past eight.
Mrs Matsumoto:	That's fine.
Agency:	So I'll check if that's OK, shall I? It's for June 9th, isn't it? And when will you be returning, Mrs Matsumoto?

Mrs Matsumoto:	A fortnight later: that's 23rd June. Can you give me the times for a flight then?
Agency:	Let's see. Er...there's a direct flight from Penang, departure time 17.30, or half past five in other words. You'd be in Hong Kong at 7.30 p.m. Would that be all right?
Mrs Matsumoto:	Perfect. Could you book that for me?
Agency:	Yes, I'll check with the airline. You'll hear from me in about an hour's time. Is that all right?
Mrs Matsumoto:	Fine. I'll be in all afternoon. Goodbye and thank you.

Task 2 🔲

Listen to the calls in Task 1 again. Decide if the following statements about the calls are true (T) or false (F).

1 The caller is considering more than one type of accommodation in Spain.   T / F
2 He doesn't think staying in Marbella is a good idea.   T / F
3 The Malaysian Airlines flight was more expensive than the Cathay Pacific one.   T / F
4 Mrs Matsumoto lives a long way from the airport.   T / F
5 Globe Travel can confirm the flight bookings immediately.   T / F

What to say – what to expect

TRAVEL ARRANGEMENTS — AIR

Person calling
Could you arrange for Mr Rogerson to be met at the airport? He's due to arrive at Paris Charles de Gaulle at 18.25 on flight BA 355.
Is there a direct flight from Dusseldorf to Geneva on Monday afternoon? I have an open ticket for this route.

Person called
I'm awfully sorry, but I couldn't get you on the flight you wanted. Your name's on the waiting list, though. The other possibility would be for you to fly at 9.00 the next morning.
We're not very conveniently located for public transport, I'm afraid.
You'd better take a taxi from the airport.

TRAVEL ARRANGEMENTS — RAIL

Person calling
I'd like a sleeper on the Inter City train from London to Glasgow.
That's right: the one that leaves Euston at 22.15 hours. It gets to Glasgow at about eight o'clock, doesn't it?

HOTEL RESERVATIONS

Person calling
Is that Advance Reservations? I'd like to reserve a double room with shower for three nights, please.
Is it a room with a view over the town?

Person called
Yes, we've booked the room you wanted. The terms are £38.50 for a single room with shower, and £45 for a double room with bath. That includes breakfast, service and value added tax.

Task 3

Choose the missing words from the box.

1 Would you like a .... room or single?
2 The .... time of flight CP 603 is 13.10.
3 Several .... fly the same route, so it's mainly a question of choosing the most .... time.
4 I want to be sure of flying tomorrow, so please book me on a .... flight.
5 Don't forget: .... time's half an hour before take-off.
6 Would you like to stay in an .... or do you prefer a hotel?
7 There are good transport .... in the area.
8 Sorry to have .... you waiting.
9 All the .... have been made. You'll be .... from us soon.
10 Shall I book hotel accommodation .... or would you .... to stay in town?

airlines	apartment	arrangements	check-in	convenient	departure
double	facilities	hearing	kept	locally	prefer	scheduled

Task 4

Choose the best answers.

1 Do you have an open ticket, then?
  a Yes, it's valid for any flight on that route.
  b Yes, I still have to pay the fare.
  c Yes, I can go anywhere in the world.

2 My name's on the waiting list as a stand-by. Can I fly now?
  a No, there's no more standing room on the plane.
  b No, the flight will be announced in the transit lounge.
  c No, the flight is fully booked.

3 Do you want to book a sleeper, or just a seat?
  a As this is a long flight, I'd like to have a sleep.
  b As this is an overnight train, I'd like to book a sleeper.
  c As this is an expensive hotel, I'd like to save some money.

4 What's the public transport like? Should I hire a car?
  a The public usually does this.
  b Trains and buses do not run frequently.
  c Trains and buses are in bad condition.

5 Is service included in the hotel rate?
  a Yes, you need not add any tips.
  b Yes, your car will be serviced while you are asleep.
  c Yes, you will be served breakfast in your room.

6 Can you reserve three single rooms for our group?

    a I'm sorry. Please ask your travel agent for fuller details.
    b I'm sorry. We don't handle package tours for groups.
    c I'm sorry. All our rooms have been reserved.

Task 5

Listen to the two telephone conversations on the cassette. While you are listening, complete the table below.

Call	Caller	Hotel location	Hotel's name	Booking	Type of room
1					
2		—			

You will find the tapescript on page 96.

What to say – what to expect

TRAVEL ARRANGEMENTS – RAIL

Person calling
Is there a dining car on the train? And can I reserve a seat there?

Person called
I'm sorry. We can't accept reservations for the dining car, but hopefully I could reserve a seat for you in an adjoining coach. Are you travelling first class or second?

TRAVEL ARRANGEMENTS – ROAD AND FERRY

Person calling / Person called
You needn't trouble to meet me. I'm hiring a car at the airport. But if you could send me a little map of how to get to your place, that'd be most useful.
The best way's to drive to Dover, take the ferry across the Channel, and then drive in the direction of Paris. It's quite easy to find our headquarters, really.

TRAVEL ARRANGEMENTS – HOTEL BOOKING

Person calling
You have a reservation for me for tomorrow. I'll be checking in rather late, I'm afraid, at about 11 p.m. You will hold the room for me, won't you?

Sorry, it looks as if I'll have to change my booking

Person called
Sorry, we're completely booked up, but you may like to try the Beach Court Hotel. This is their phone number.
We haven't any double rooms left but I can offer you a suite at £60 a night.
I'm awfully sorry, there are no hotel rooms left. Shall I look for private

Something urgent has happened, so I've had to change my plans.

accommodation for you, or try to find a hotel out of town?
Would you mind sending me written confirmation?

Task 6 🔲

Listen to the next two telephone calls on the cassette. While you are listening to the first one, complete the telexes below.

1
```
63461 WEALD G
92730 SODER S
4 APRIL 1986

ATTN MR BENGTSSON

THANKS FOR YOUR LETTER OF (1) ....... GLAD TO WELCOME YOU
HERE (2) ...... PLEASE BE OUR GUEST AT (3) ....... THAT
EVENING. WOULD YOU LIKE A HOTEL IN LONDON OR (4) .......?
WEALDS IS 45 MINUTES BY TRAIN FROM LONDON OR BY TAXI FROM
THE AIRPORT.

THOMPSON WEALD
```

2
```
92730 SODER S
63461 WEALD G
4 APRIL 1986

ATTN MR THOMPSON

GRATEFUL FOR YOUR ASSISTANCE. PLS BOOK ME INTO HOTEL IN
WATFORD (5) ....... APRIL, AND NOTIFY ME OF ADDRESS AND
(6) .......

BENGTSSON
```

3
```
63461 WEALD G
92730 SODER S
5 APRIL 1986

ATTN MR BENGTSSON

HAVE RESERVED HOTEL ACCOMMODATION AT (7) ......., 3 EEE 2
HARROW ROAD, WATFORD, NEAR THE (8) ......., TELEPHONE
(9) .......SHALL CALL FOR YOU (10) ....... MONDAY AND
LOOK FORWARD TO SEEING YOU.

THOMPSON WEALD
```

You will find the tapescript on pages 97–98

Task 7 🖭

Listening check

1 What difficulties did Matthew Sharp encounter during his trip?
2 What difficulties does this cause Weald's?
3 Which two places is Matthew Sharp visiting in one day?
4 Why does Pat Thompson want Sharp to ring him back?

Task 8

Complete the following conversation with phrases from the list below. Use each phrase only once.

Scandinavian Airlines. Good morning.
1 ....
2 ....
Flight Reservations.
3 ....
How can we help you, Mr Rogerson?
4 ....
I see.
5 ....
You're flying full economy fare, I suppose?
6 ....
Well, in that case, if there's a seat available on the plane, you'll have no problem.
7 ....
8 ....
Is the summer departure time very different, then?
9 ....
That's still very convenient.
10 ....
Yes, please.
Right, go to the SAS desk at the airport at least 60 minutes before departure.
11 ....
Yes, it's YA 712.
12 ....
Bye.

a But my conference is ending earlier and I'd like to take an earlier flight back.
b Hold the line, sir, and I'll put you through to Flight Reservations.
c And there are a few seats left. Shall I reserve one for you?
d SK 512 is the flight that interests me. The one at 16.35.
e That's fine, then. Thanks very much. Bye.
f Good morning. I'd like to change a flight booking, please.
g Ah, good morning, my name's Rogerson.
h And they'll change the ticket, then? Is there a reference number?
i No, only 20 minutes later. At 16.55.
j Well, I'm booked on a Swissair flight to Zurich this Friday at 18.40.
k Yes, I am.
l I think your timetable must be out of date, sir. That's the winter departure time.

LANGUAGE STUDY

Task 9 Probability and possibility

We often use *will*, *should* and *might* when we want to show how certain we are about what we are saying.

more certain	certain	The Managing Director *will* chair the meeting.
	probable	Mr Jones *should* be back this afternoon.
	possible	I *might* meet him later.

Now change the following sentences to show how certain you are.

Example:
Their order is likely to arrive tomorrow.
   Their order **should** arrive tomorrow.

1 I'm not sure if we will visit Sao Paulo on the way home.
2 It's likely that the goods will reach you by the end of the week.
3 You will probably get a good discount from the car company.
4 The discount is certain to be bigger if you order over 1000 units.
5 The reference number is probably at the top of the page.
6 He's certain to ring you before 12 tomorrow.

Task 10 Reporting questions

When you pass on a message, you will need to report three types of questions.

'Is he satisfied with the discount?' (*He asked*)
   He asked **if/whether** you **were** satisfied with the discount.
'Why haven't you delivered my order?' (*He wanted to know*)
   He wanted to know **why** we **hadn't** delivered his order.
'What will the discount be? (*He wanted to know*)
   He wanted to know **what** the discount **would** be.

Now report the following questions in a similar way.

 1 'Is the order firm?' (*They wanted to know*)
 2 'What is the reference number?' (*He asked me*)
 3 'Is there a bigger discount for larger orders?' (*He inquired*)
 4 'Where have you filed the records?' (*She asked me*)
 5 'When will the goods reach us?' (*He wondered*)
 6 'Do you expect to receive the goods soon?' (*He asked me*)
 7 'How long do I have to wait?' (*She asked me*)
 8 'Have you booked your flight yet?' (*She wanted to know*)
 9 'Can I pay by credit card?' (*She wondered*)
10 'Where will the goods be delivered?' (*He wanted to know*)

SPEAKING

Task 11 📼

He's German, *isn't he*? Question tags like this can be pronounced in two ways. If they are spoken with a rising tone (⤴), they are real questions. If they are spoken with a falling tone (⤵), they confirm information. Listen to the examples and then add question tags to the sentences below. Check that the tone rises or falls correctly.

1 It's twenty past ten.   (⤴)
2 You're going to the Berlin Fair.   (⤵)
3 She's already paid.   (⤵)
4 You can meet them.   (⤴)
5 They haven't called us back.   (⤵)
6 There's a 10% discount.   (⤴)
7 That's the reference number.   (⤵)
8 They can't take another thousand.   (⤴)

Task 12 📼

You work for Mr Thompson at Weald. He receives the following telex from Mr Bengtsson cancelling his visit. Mr Thompson asks you to telephone the hotel to cancel the reservation.

```
92730 SODER S
63461 WEALD G
7 APRIL 1986


FOR PERSONAL REASONS MUST CANCEL UK TRIP.
PLS CANCEL HOTEL FOR 9/10 APRIL.

RGDS BENGTSSON
```

Task 13   Role play

Work with another student when you do this exercise. Student B has information on this page, student A on page 106.

B1 You work for Rentacar Ltd. Your smallest cars cost £12 per day, plus £3 per day insurance and then £2.25 in tax. You have no special weekend arrangements.

B2 You work for Cheaprent Ltd. Your cars cost £18, £27 and £36 per day for the small, medium and large sizes respectively. The prices are inclusive, except for petrol. You also do inclusive weekend arrangements at £29, £39 and £49.

B3 You work for Interworld Travel, London. The flight the caller would like is full and there are 17 people on the waiting list. Offer the caller, as alternatives, BA 314 at 20.00 or British Caledonian (BR 106) at 19.20 from London's Gatwick Airport.

TELECOM SERVICES

Task 14   Text communication

The following (adapted) text is from Facts about Televerket (Swedish Telecom) 1985. Read it and decide if the six statements below it are true or false.

Telegrams

During the last 20 years telegram traffic has been steadily falling. Domestic telegrams during the financial year 1983/84 numbered 445,000. The number of telegrams to and from other countries was 315,000.

Telex

The total number of telex subscriptions in Sweden amounts today to approximately 18,000 and there are, looking at the world as a whole, more than one and a half million subscribers in more than 190 countries. The Swedish telex service has undergone a complete modernisation. Thanks to the introduction of electronic telex exchanges, AXB 20, customers have access to a number of new services, e.g. TELEX 080, abbreviated dialling and specified charging. Via TELEX 080 messages are automatically transmitted to the called subscriber and at the desired time.

Telefax

The telefax service makes it possible to send and receive text, diagrams, pictures etc using a telefax set. Televerket's telefax sets are directly connected to the telephone network. At the end of 1984 there were about 10,000 telefax terminals. The terminals supplied by Televerket are technically very advanced. The time for transmitting a DIN A4 page is almost always less than a minute.

Using the Telefax

Teletex

The Teletex service in Sweden went into commercial operation in 1983. Teletex offers important advantages over the telex service. There is, for example, access to word and text processing facilities and the character set corresponds to that of a standard typewriter. Transmission is rapid. The text on an A4 size sheet of paper can be transmitted in less than 10 seconds. Intercommunication with telex is possible.

1 For every international telegram, more than two domestic telegrams are sent and received.   T/F
2 The Swedish telex service is being modernised.   T/F
3 Telefax sets are connected to the telephone network.   T/F
4 Word processing is possible on telex terminals.   T/F
5 Telex messages can be sent to teletex terminals.   T/F

6 LET'S FIX ANOTHER DATE

LISTENING

Task 1 📼

Listen to the next two telephone calls on the cassette. While you are listening, complete the table below.

Call	Caller	Person called	Original appointment	Reason for change	New arrangement
1					
2					

Unit 6 *Let's fix another date*

CHANGING AN APPOINTMENT

Andrew Brickwood:	071 34541.
Bob Ross:	Bob Ross here. Could I speak to Mr Brickwood, please?
Andrew Brickwood:	Speaking.
Bob Ross:	Oh, it's you, Andrew, is it? I didn't recognise your voice. Sounds as if you're miles away.
Andrew Brickwood:	Oh, hello, Bob. Yes, the line isn't very good. I'll speak a bit louder. Is that any better?
Bob Ross:	Yes, that's much better now. Andrew, it looks as if I won't be able to keep the appointment we made.
Andrew Brickwood:	That was to be Friday, wasn't it?
Bob Ross:	Yes, I'm so sorry. This visitor I was actually expecting last week had some kind of change in his itinerary, and now he's rung me up to say the only day he can come is next Friday.
Andrew Brickwood:	I see.
Bob Ross:	And the trouble is, as he's over from Argentina, I can't very well put him off. Hope you understand.
Andrew Brickwood:	Well, I suppose so.
Bob Ross:	But could we meet on Saturday? Or would you prefer the beginning of next week?
Andrew Brickwood:	Afraid I'm tied up at the weekend. And ... let me just check. No, Monday's not too good a day either. Tuesday would be all right, I think.
Bob Ross:	Tuesday's OK for me too. Oh good. Shall we say the same time as we'd arranged? Could you come here at 11.30? I'll show you round our place, we could lunch together and work out the terms of our contract in the afternoon. How does that sound to you?
Andrew Brickwood:	Yes, fine. I'll just note it down in my diary. That's Tuesday 12th June. Right, I'll be at your place at 11.30 then, Bob.
Bob Ross:	Thanks, Andrew. Hope I haven't messed up your arrangements too much.
Andrew Brickwood:	Oh no, these things happen, don't they? See you next Tuesday, Bob. And have a nice weekend.
Bob Ross:	Thanks. You too, Andrew. Bye.

EXCUSES FOR NOT ATTENDING A MEETING

Mr Masterton:	713 2092. Masterton speaking.
Ann Perkins:	Morning, Mr Masterton. Ann Perkins here.
Mr Masterton:	Ah, Miss Perkins. This is an unexpected pleasure. Can I help you in any way? We're seeing each other tomorrow, aren't we?
Ann Perkins:	That's just what I'm phoning about. I've got 'flu, it seems, so I can't attend the board meeting after all.
Mr Masterton:	Oh, isn't that too bad! We've got some important things to discuss, too. About the pension plan, and those other points.
Ann Perkins:	Exactly. Now this is what I'd like to suggest ... just an idea it is, but I'd like you to tell me what you think of it. Oh, just a moment ... Excuse me.
Mr Masterton:	Bless you!
Ann Perkins:	Thanks. My assistant – that's Martin Close – he's very well informed on this subject. I thought of asking him to go to the

60

	meeting in my place. You know, he and I drafted these new pension plan regulations for our employees, so he really knows what they're all about.
Mr Masterton:	Have you asked Harold Foster? He's chairing the meeting, of course.
Ann Perkins:	No, I thought I'd check with you first. If you think it's an acceptable solution, I'll get on to Mr Foster. You see the other alternative would be to send you my notes, perhaps, and you could put forward my ideas.
Mr Masterton:	No, no, I don't think so. I mean of course I'd be quite glad to do so, but if there were any questions involved I would hardly be in a position to answer them, whereas your Mr Martin could ...
Ann Perkins:	Yes, that was what I thought. Er ... Mr Close, it is ... Martin's his first name.
Mr Masterton:	Ah yes, Martin Close. Well, I think that's the best thing. Let him come to the meeting in your place. I'm sure the chairman will agree to that.
Ann Perkins:	Right, I'll contact him. But I'm glad I've spoken to you about it.
Mr Masterton:	So am I. I hope you get well soon. Goodbye, Miss Perkins.
Ann Perkins:	Goodbye, Mr Masterton.

Task 2

Decide if the following sentences are true (T) or false (F).

1 Bob Ross didn't recognise Andrew Brickwood's voice because he was miles away. T/F
2 Bob Ross can't change his other appointment because his visitor lives a long way away. T/F
3 Both of them are busy all weekend. T/F
4 Mr Close and Miss Perkins had together prepared the material for the meeting. T/F
5 Miss Perkins considered sending her notes instead of Mr Close. T/F
6 Mr Masterton thinks he would be able to answer questions about the pension plan. T/F

What to say – what to expect

MAKING APPOINTMENTS

Person calling/Person called
I'll just check my appointment book.
When would be convenient for you?
Sorry, I've got something scheduled then. Could we arrange something else?
Could you send me confirmation of the appointment?
Shall we say Wednesday at 3 o'clock?
Would it be possible to postpone our meeting?
Things are going smoothly, so we can meet as arranged.

Task 3

Choose the missing words from the box.

1. I can hardly .... your voice. It's as if you're miles ....
2. My visitor couldn't keep to his ...., and now I must change my ....
3. Let me just look at my .... Yes, I could come next Monday.
4. So sorry, I'll be .... then.
5. I'm afraid I can't .... the meeting we'd arranged.
6. The .... of the conference are to .... our new products and explain our ....
7. No, I'm not the chairman, but I'll act as his ....
8. You arranged things so well that everything ran ....
9. Can you see that the .... are installed for us?
10. Make sure you remember everything: it's best to make a ....

appointments	attend	away	checklist	delegate	describe
diary	itinerary	loudspeakers	objectives	recognise	services
smoothly	tied up				

Task 4

Choose the best responses.

1. Can we make an appointment?
   a When are you free?
   b Shall we make a reservation?
   c Is it difficult for us to meet?

2. I'm tied up on Monday and Tuesday.
   a What about Wednesday?
   b I'll come on Monday, then.
   c Oh, I'm sorry to hear it.

3. Has this messed up your arrangements again?
   a My desk is always in a mess.
   b These things happen.
   c Yes, I always arrange things like this.

4. Did the conference run smoothly?
   a Yes, we finished much later than usual.
   b Yes, it went very quickly.
   c Yes, there were no problems. It was well organised.

5. I've drafted the letter to Ms Clayton.
   a Oh good, I'll send it this morning.
   b Right, I'll check it straight away.
   c Did you keep a top copy?

6. Can you get on to Mr Foster about the report?
   a Yes, I'll send him a copy.
   b I'll ring him immediately.
   c I'll tell him when I see him.

Task 5 🔊

Listen to the two telephone conversations on the cassette. While you are listening, complete the table below.

Call	Caller	Person called	Reason for calling	Appointment
1				
2				

You will find the tapescript on pages 98–99.

What to say – what to expect

CHANGING APPOINTMENTS

Person calling/Person called
Could you manage to fix another appointment?
How about the 4th? Are you free then?
So sorry I missed you when you wanted to visit me. I was away all week and only got your message too late.
I'm phoning you because I don't think I'll be able to come after all.
Let's fix another date then. Would it suit you if we met at the club on Friday afternoon?

Task 6 🔊

Listen to the next two telephone conversations on the cassette. Take notes on each of the calls. In the first, imagine you are Susan Shields and in the second, Jim Harris.

1

2

Notes

You will find the tapescript on pages 99–100

Task 7 🔲

Listening check

1 Why is Pat Thompson phoning Susan Shields about the conference?
2 What are the objectives of the conference?
3 What's the disadvantage of the Northwest Conference Hall?
4 Why hasn't Mr Harris heard of Weald?
5 Why would Pat Thompson like Mr Harris to speak at the conference?

Task 8

Complete the following conversation with phrases from the list on the next page.

1 ....
Not bad at all. You, Richard?
2 ....
Well, we're sending a news team to do a story on Central America.
3 ....
You guessed!
4 ....
From about the middle to the end of next month.
5 ....
That's right.
6 ....
That's really good news.
7 ....
What's the problem? We'll pay you your normal rate.
8 ....
And then you'll confirm?
9 ....
I'll do that, Richard. Hope it all goes well.
10 ....
Bye now.

a Can't complain. What can I do for you?
b Hold on a minute. It's not definite yet.
c I'm sure it will. Thanks for calling, Pete.
d No, it's not that. I'll have to make some arrangements first.
e Peter, good to hear from you. How are things?
f About two weeks, then?
g When would the journey be?
h Yes, that should be OK.
i Yes, if I haven't confirmed by the end of next week, get in touch again.
j Let me guess. You need a cameraman.

LANGUAGE STUDY

Task 9 *Considering future possibilities*

Examples:
What *would happen* if Cheryl Nelson *wasn't offered* the job? (*she/apply/elsewhere*)
   If Cheryl Nelson **wasn't offered** the job, she **would apply** elsewhere.
What *would happen* if you *couldn't keep* the appointment? (*I/telephone/apologise*)
   I **would telephone** and apologise if I **couldn't keep** the appointment.

1 What would be the result if Weald's products were not well advertised?
   (*their sales/fall*)
   If ....
2 What would be the effect if your supplier stopped your discount?
   (*we/consider/using another supplier*)
   We ....
3 What would happen if the speaker couldn't come to the conference?
   (*we/look for/replacement*)
   If ....
4 What would you do if the TWA flight was cancelled?
   (*I/book/another airline*)
   I ....
5 What would be the result if your market share decreased suddenly?
   (*there/be/drop in revenue*)
   There ....
6 What would be the result if the value of the pound fell?
   (*Weald's exports/be/more competitively priced*)
   If ....

Task 10 *Using nouns in groups*

Complete the list.

A pad for messages   → a message pad
A telephone with buttons that you press → a press-button telephone
A number for reference   → 1 ....
2 ....   → number unobtainable tone

65

Code for the area of York	→ 3 ....
A system for connecting calls	→ 4 ....
5	→ electronic text communication system
dialling trunk (calls) by subscribers	→ 6 ....
7	→ Boston Symphony Orchestra
8	→ 3-digit country codes
A system for reserving seats with airlines	→ 9 ....
10	→ 6-minute Monday lunch-time call

SPEAKING

Task 11 🔲

Listen to the callers on the cassette. They will ask you for some information which is given below.

1 27 September 1985
2 A/7912–FJ
3 Kristiansand
4 009 44 43486 293
5 Piet Boonstra

6 19 200 bits/second
7 S-C-A-N-D-A-T-A AB
8 10.45 a.m. 18 August
9 Ciudad Guyana
10 010 9 72 3 635400

Task 12 🔲

Here is a page from your diary for 27th June. Bob Logan telephones to change the 10 a.m. meeting because he has a dentist's appointment. He wants to arrange another meeting.

	27 June Tuesday
9.00	Phone Delhi office
10.00	Bob Logan
11.00	Sally Parker/Oscar Novak – publicity
12.00	↓
1.00	Lunch with Sergio Rames
2.00	Warehouse
3.00	
4.00	Sales meeting Rm 259
5.00	↓

Task 13   Role play

Work with another student when you do this exercise. Student B has information on this page, student A on page 106.

B1 You are Derek Hodgson, British Telecom's Euronet manager. You are very interested in the data communications equipment manufactured by the company the person who calls you represents. You would very much like to meet the caller. Try to arrange a meeting. Here is the relevant page from your appointment diary.

WEEK 48					
MONDAY	TUESDAY	WEDNESDAY	THURSDAY	FRIDAY	
Sales meeting					9
					10
	Planning group	Leave for airport	CCITT working party Data communication standards		11
					12
		13.15 BA 614 to Geneva			13
Prepare planning report			Geneva		14
					15
				15.45 SR 312 to London	16
	Theatre 8				EVE

B2 You are Professor Patricia Malcolm, a specialist in market research techniques. You have given keynote speeches before, normally for a fee of about £350 plus travel expenses.

TELECOM SERVICES

Task 14

Look at the instructions for using a payphone and then answer the questions below.

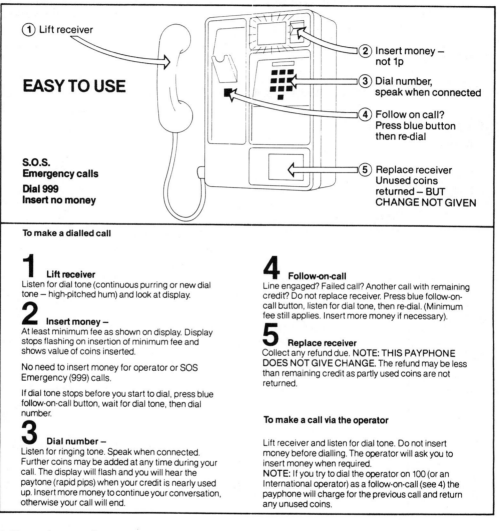

① Lift receiver

EASY TO USE

S.O.S.
Emergency calls

Dial 999
Insert no money

② Insert money –
not 1p

③ Dial number,
speak when connected

④ Follow on call?
Press blue button
then re-dial

⑤ Replace receiver
Unused coins
returned – BUT
CHANGE NOT GIVEN

To make a dialled call

1 Lift receiver
Listen for dial tone (continuous purring or new dial tone – high-pitched hum) and look at display.

2 Insert money –
At least minimum fee as shown on display. Display stops flashing on insertion of minimum fee and shows value of coins inserted.

No need to insert money for operator or SOS Emergency (999) calls.

If dial tone stops before you start to dial, press blue follow-on-call button, wait for dial tone, then dial number.

3 Dial number –
Listen for ringing tone. Speak when connected. Further coins may be added at any time during your call. The display will flash and you will hear the paytone (rapid pips) when your credit is nearly used up. Insert more money to continue your conversation, otherwise your call will end.

4 Follow-on-call
Line engaged? Failed call? Another call with remaining credit? Do not replace receiver. Press blue follow-on-call button, listen for dial tone, then re-dial. (Minimum fee still applies. Insert more money if necessary).

5 Replace receiver
Collect any refund due. NOTE: THIS PAYPHONE DOES NOT GIVE CHANGE. The refund may be less than remaining credit as partly used coins are not returned.

To make a call via the operator

Lift receiver and listen for dial tone. Do not insert money before dialling. The operator will ask you to insert money when required.
NOTE: If you try to dial the operator on 100 (or an International operator) as a follow-on-call (see 4) the payphone will charge for the previous call and return any unused coins.

1 Does the payphone accept every kind of coin?
2 What happens when you need to insert more money?
3 If you still have credit and wish to make a second call, what should you do?
4 How many types of call can you make without inserting money?

7 WHAT SEEMS TO BE THE TROUBLE?

LISTENING

Task 1 🎝

Listen to the telephone calls on the cassette. While you are listening, take notes using the message pads below. In the first call, you are the operator and in the second one you are Mr MacDougall.

1

    Telephone Message

    To _____

    From _____
    _____
    _____
    _____
    _____

    Date _____ Signed _____

2

    _____
    _____
    _____
    _____
    _____
    _____
    _____
    _____
    _____
    _____

AN URGENT CALL

Operator:	Whitehill, Inverness.
Mr Janssen:	Hello, I'm calling from Holland. This is the Janssen Company of Hilversum. Is Mr MacDougall there?
Operator:	Well, yes he is here, but he's on another line. Hold the line, please, and I'll tell him you're calling.
Mr Janssen:	Yes, if you would. It's urgent.
Operator:	Excuse me, Mr MacDougall, there's an urgent call from Holland. Could you take it please? It's Mr Janssen.
Mr MacDougall:	Oh, could you tell him I'll call him back in a few minutes?
Operator:	Mr Janssen, can Mr MacDougall ring you back in about five minutes' time?
Mr Janssen:	Oh, all right – if it's not longer. I'm only in till 11 o'clock.
Operator:	Right, Mr Janssen, I've made a note of that. That's 12 o'clock our time. I'm sure he'll call you well before then. The number's 3135 789280, isn't it?
Mr Janssen:	Yes, that's it. So long.
Operator:	Goodbye, Mr Janssen.

A COMPLAINT

Mr MacDougall:	MacDougall of Whitehill here, returning Mr Janssen's call.
Mr Janssen:	Oh, hello, Mr MacDougall. Wim Janssen here. I'm glad you rang back so soon. There's a serious problem, I'm afraid. You know that order for 600 cases of Whitehill Malt Whisky we put in recently?
Mr MacDougall:	Oh yes, I saw to it myself. What's the problem. Hasn't it arrived?
Mr Janssen:	Well, in a way, but it's got stuck at the customs. There's something wrong with the declaration, it seems. Some kind of omission or error.
Mr MacDougall:	Oh, really? That's strange. D'you know what it is?
Mr Janssen:	Well, I only heard that some of the details were incomplete and the customs can't let the consignment through.
Mr MacDougall:	Mr Janssen, I'll tell you what I'll do. Our forwarding agents are handling this delivery and they're generally very reliable. Er … let me just get on to them.
Mr Janssen:	Yes, if you would. And can you let me know as soon as possible when I can have the whisky? Time's rather short, you know.
Mr MacDougall:	Of course. I'll see to it, Mr Janssen, and if at all possible, you'll get a call today.
Mr Janssen:	Well, getting the delivery today would suit me better. Oh, one other thing. I'm out of the office after 12 o'clock, your time, so would you leave a message with our switchboard operator. I'll tell her to expect your call.
Mr MacDougall:	Yes, I spoke to her before. I'll get things moving as quickly as I can.
Mr Janssen:	Right. Thanks. Goodbye then, Mr MacDougall.
Mr MacDougall:	Goodbye. You'll be hearing from us very soon.

Task 2

Decide if the following sentences are true (T) or false (F).

1 Mr Janssen has his own company.	T/F
2 Mr Janssen agrees to call back in a few minutes.	T/F
3 The order was for 600 bottles of malt whisky.	T/F
4 The customs are holding the whisky because they need more information.	T/F
5 Mr MacDougall is going to contact the customs.	T/F
6 The whisky will be delivered today.	T/F

What to say – what to expect

MAKING AND RECEIVING COMPLAINTS

Person calling
I'm afraid I have to make/register a
   serious complaint.
I'm returning the machine to you by air
   freight.
I must make a complaint about the
   service at your hotel.
You may think I'm a nuisance, or that
   I'm too fussy, but I really can't accept
   this kind of thing again.
The taxi came so late that I missed my
   flight to Rome.

Person called
I'm afraid there's been a mix-up.
What seems to be the trouble?
When did you place the order?

Task 3

Choose the missing words from the box.

1 I'm phoning you about a .... matter; in fact, it's extremely ....
2 The .... hasn't reached us yet.
3 It must have been .... during transport.
4 You don't need to do anything. The .... are dealing with the delivery.
5 Surely it's your department that .... the orders beforehand?
6 Yes, but certain things may go .... in any business.
7 Of course, we do everything we can to avoid a ...., though there may be difficulties sometimes.
8 We're very .... to .... you.

consignment	delayed	forwarding agents	inconvenience
mix-up	processes	serious	sorry	urgent	wrong

Task 4

Choose the best responses.

1 The consignment's got stuck at the customs.
   a So we can collect it, can we?
   b Why has it been delayed?
   c You mean they've stamped it.

2 Our forwarding agents will handle it.
   a It's very fragile.
   b Will they be here soon?
   c Are they reliable?

3 I'll get on to them.
   a If you would.
   b When can you go?
   c If you see them, tell them.

4 I'll call you tomorrow. Would 12.30 suit you?
   a Yes, I go to lunch at 12.
   b Yes, it would be a bit difficult then.
   c 12.30 would be fine.

5 I'll get things moving as quickly as I can.
   a The sooner you go, the better.
   b I'd appreciate that.
   c Don't move them without telling me.

6 There's been a bit of a mix-up.
   a What's the problem?
   b Why did you disturb it?
   c I'm sorry everything is in the wrong place.

Task 5

Listen to the next two telephone conversations on the cassette. While you are listening, complete the table below.

Call	Caller	Person called	Company called	Reason for complaint
1				
2				

You will find the tapescript on pages 100–101.

What to say – what to expect

MAKING AND RECEIVING COMPLAINTS

Person calling
They're not like the samples we got. The quality just isn't good enough.
Of course I understand that there may be a delay, but can't you please let us

Person called
Yes, I did report the accident on the day it happened, but you didn't tell me on the phone that I had to send in a written report too.

know. Then we can plan accordingly.

I wish you'd keep to the deadlines we fixed. The parts I ordered for last week still haven't arrived.

But you told us we could count on delivery by the 21st and it was only on that condition that we placed the order.

Listen, I haven't got time to wait for your 'full investigation'. When am I going to get full compensation? That's what I want to know.

Look, I realise this may put you in a difficult position, but I think it's better for you to know exactly how things stand.

Task 6

Listen to the next two telephone conversations on the cassette. Take notes on each of the calls. Imagine you are Mr Graham in the first and Fred Lucas in the second.

1

WEALD
of Watford

2

WEALD
of Watford

You will find the tapescript on pages 101–102.

Task 7 📼

Listening check

1 Why is Mr Tomlin angry?
2 Which department does the operator connect him with?
3 How can Mr Graham trace what has gone wrong?
4 How will he find out about the delivery?
5 When he's found out, what will he do?
6 How does Fred handle the complaint?
7 What is the cause of the mix-up?
8 What solution does Mr Graham suggest?
9 What does Fred need in order to set things straight?
10 When can Fred send off the tennis shoes Tomlin Sport want?

Task 8

Complete the following conversation with phrases from the list below.

1 ....
Good morning. Could you put me through to Keith Sharp, please?
2 ....
Oh dear. Do you know when he'll be back?
3 ....
Well, I'm afraid I'm having problems with some of your components.
4 ....
Yes, that sounds promising.
5 ....
Bob Jackman, Technical Liaison.
6 ....
Good morning, Mr Lepic. How can I help you?
7 ....
Do you have the code numbers for the ICs, Mr Lepic?
8 ....
That's the new range, I believe.
9 ....
What seems to be the problem with them?
10 ....

a I'll put you through to Bob Jackman.
b I'm afraid he's away on a business trip.
c Yes, they're all from the IC/GA/1764 range.
d Ah hello, my name's Pierre Lepic from Autelec in Paris.
e They're fine except when the ambient temperature drops below . . .
f Medway Electronics. Good morning.
g Not until next week, I'm afraid. Can somebody else help you?
h That's right.
i Well, I bought some integrated circuits from you and . . .
j I see. Technical Liaison should be able to help you.

LANGUAGE STUDY

Task 9 *Apologising*

It is sometimes necessary to apologise because someone has not done something that they *should have done*. Look at this example.

The consignment was delayed at the customs. (*send/more information*)
   *I'm sorry. We **should have sent** more information.*

Apologise in a similar way for the following.

1 Two of the three boxes were wrong. (*label/correctly*)
2 The circuits don't work below 10°C. (*tell/about that*)
3 You sent me the wrong recorder. (*check/your order*)
4 I missed my connection to Miami. (*give/more exact information*)
5 The restaurant was full. (*reserve/table*)
6 There was no instruction manual. (*put/in the box*)

Task 10 *Getting things done*

You will often need to say that you will get another person to perform a service for the person you are talking to. This is how you can do it.

The car you lent me is not working well. (*service*)
   *I'll **have it serviced** for you.*

1 Are you sure this invoice is correct? (*check*)
2 The photocopier isn't working too well. (*fix*)
3 There may be some letters for me. (*forward*)
4 I'd like some information about the XT-12. (*send*)
5 I need those parts as soon as possible. (*dispatch at once*)
6 I've left my papers in the top office. (*bring down*)

SPEAKING

Task 11 📼

Study the table below and then say the following figures and calculations aloud. Then listen to the cassette to check that you have said them correctly.

=	equals, is equal to, makes, is	1204	one thousand two hundred and four
+	plus, and	$\frac{3}{4}$	three quarters
−	minus, less, take away	$\frac{2}{3}$	two thirds
×	times, multiplied by	1·204	one point two oh four
÷	divided by	$\frac{3}{8}$	three eighths

1   $\frac{1}{2} + \frac{3}{4} = 1\frac{1}{4}$ 6 $10 \div 2 = 5$
2   27·139   7 $\frac{11}{16} - \frac{3}{8} = \frac{5}{16}$
3   $4·2 \times 3 = 12·6$ 8 $12\frac{2}{3}\%$
4   11·5%   9   1·712
5   27 139   10 $96 + 24 - 13 = 107$

Task 12 📼

You work for Johnson Brothers. Here is a copy of an order you sent to Packard Enterprises and the invoice you have just received. You are now speaking to Ms McLeod of Customer Services to complain. You may listen to the cassette first to help you.

Johnson Brothers

I4 May
Order no 4102

Please supply:
13 Model MS 302 clips
at 15p

For Johnson Brothers

Packard for Parts

26 June
Invoice no 6597

To Johnson Bros
Re your order no 4102

30 Model MS 302
clips @ 15p

£4.50

Task 13   Role play

Work with another student when you do this exercise. Student B has information on this page, student A on pages 106–107.

B1 You are the Room Service Manager at the Bristol Hotel. Apologise to the customer for the mistakes and explain that you are short of staff and that the mistakes are because of this. Tell the customer you'll have things fixed as soon as possible.

B2 You are the Customer Liaison Manager for Brown Trading Ltd. Explain to the caller that the F13 is the de luxe version of the F12 and that it has all the features of the F12. Also explain that your publicity material in English is being reprinted. You thought it was better to send something in German than nothing at all. Say that you will send what is required as soon as you can.

B3 You work for Kowloon Travel Services in Hong Kong. Help the customer who rings you.

TELECOM SERVICES

Task 14

Read the passage about telephone meetings and TV conferences and answer the questions which follow.

In the 1970s a number of telecommunications administrations introduced a new idea: telephone meetings or conferences by telephone. The form of the conference depends on the number of participants and where they are located. When a number of people in different locations are involved, a multiple, or conference call is needed. When there is a group of people in one location, they use a loudspeaking telephone or a conference telephone with headsets (see below). The idea of telephone instead of personal meetings is to avoid travel expenses and time lost while travelling. The disadvantage of such meetings is that you can neither see the other people involved nor show any visual material. This is overcome when a conference TV service is used. The comparison below is one that Swedish Telecom made in 1981.

Alternative A	**Alternative B**
Three people fly from Luleå to Stockholm for a meeting from 9 to 12 am. The outward journey is made the day before. Three participants are from Stockholm.	The three Luleå participants remain in Luleå and set up the meeting as a TV conference.

Conventional meeting	(Costs are in US $)	**TV meeting**
$554	Travel costs for Luleå participants	$5
—	Travel costs for Stockholm participants	$12
$44	Allowable flat-rate expenses	—
$120	Hotel accommodation	—
—	Charge for TV meeting	$450
27 hours	Man-hours between 8am and 5pm for Luleå group	11 hours
9 hours	Man-hours between 8am and 5pm for Stockholm group	11 hours
42 hours	Man-hours outside above time for Luleå group	—
—	Cost saving (no allowance for time saving)	$251
—	Cost saving (hours between 8am and 5pm) valued at $20	$531
—	Time saving for TV meeting	56 man-hours

1 When are multiple calls required?
2 When is a conference or loudspeaking telephone needed?
3 What is the aim of telephone meetings?
4 Why are there travel costs in Alternative B?
5 What is the hotel rate per person per night in the example?
6 What is the disadvantage of the conference TV service for people who live in small or medium-sized towns?

8 I'M SURE WE CAN SORT IT OUT

LISTENING

Task 1

Listen to the next two telephone calls on the cassette. While you are listening, complete the table below.

Call	Caller	Called person/company	Reason for calling	Action	Next contact
1					
2					

NON-PAYMENT OF BILL

Reliance:	Reliance Mail Order Company here. Is that Mr Bronson?
Edward Bronson:	Speaking.
Reliance:	Good morning, Mr Bronson. I'm sorry to disturb you. We don't usually phone customers about overdue payments, but we have, in fact, written to you twice.
Edward Bronson:	Written to me twice? What on earth about?
Reliance:	It's about the bicycle we sent you. You did get it all right, didn't you?
Edward Bronson:	Oh that. Yes, I did. Now I know who you are. Yes, I got the bicycle and I think I've paid for it too.
Reliance:	Sorry, Mr Bronson, that's what I'm ringing about. We haven't received a cheque from you.
Edward Bronson:	No, I didn't pay by cheque. I gave my bank instructions to make a transfer.
Reliance:	Well, there may have been a slip at our end, but according to our records, nothing's come in. Could I ask you to check with your bank and let me know exactly when the remittance was made, you know, date, which bank, how it was transferred and so on. I'm sure we'll be able to trace it then.
Edward Bronson:	OK, I'll do that. Yes, I think I've got your bill somewhere.
Reliance:	We could send you a duplicate if you like.
Edward Bronson:	Oh yes, would you do that? Then I'll look into it right away. I . . . I'm sure we can sort it out.
Reliance:	Right. Then we'll get a notification from you.
Edward Bronson:	From me or my bank. I'll see to it. Goodbye then.
Reliance:	Thanks, Mr Bronson. Goodbye.

AN AIR PASSENGER HAS PROBLEMS

Flyway:	Flyway Airlines. Good morning.
Carlos Rodríguez:	Hello. My name is Carlos Rodríguez. I didn't get my luggage when I arrived here yesterday.
Flyway:	Yes, sir. I'll put you on to our Lost and Found Office. Just a second, please.
Lost and found:	Lost and Found Office. Can I help you?
Carlos Rodríguez:	I certainly hope so. I flew here from Toronto yesterday, but when I arrived my luggage was missing.
Lost and found:	Oh dear! Did you report it when you landed?
Carlos Rodríguez:	Yes, I told them at the information office but I didn't have time to contact you too. I had a business meeting to attend. It's a damned nuisance this and it isn't the first time either.
Lost and found:	Mr Rodríguez, I'll try to find out where your luggage is, but I do need some information from you. What flight was it and what time did you arrive at the airport?
Carlos Rodríguez:	It was flight FL 879 and I had a two-hour stopover in New York. The plane was almost an hour late so we landed at about nine o'clock yesterday morning.
Lost and found:	Fine, I also need to know the number of your baggage check, Mr Rodríguez. You'll find it on the front of your ticket.
Carlos Rodríguez:	Why can't you people do anything without masses of numbers

	and things? I suppose there'll be forms and declarations that I'll have to fill in.
Lost and found:	No, that won't be necessary. I'm sorry, I realise it must be annoying, but you see there are hundreds of passengers passing through here every day, so there has to be some system.
Carlos Rodríguez:	OK, OK. Here's the number of the baggage check. It's FL 052273 and 052274. A small case and a large one. Both in dark brown leather.
Lost and found:	Thank you, Mr Rodríguez. Now I'll be able to trace your missing luggage. If you give me your phone number, I'll call you back.
Carlos Rodríguez:	Right. It's 5691273 until four o'clock and after that you can reach me, or leave a message, at the Grand Hotel. The number's …
Lost and found:	That's OK, Mr Rodríguez, we've got the number. I do hope we can get your bags to you this evening or tomorrow. If it's not today, I'll give you a call where you are now or at your hotel.
Carlos Rodríguez:	Fine. Please do your best to make it today. It really is quite difficult for me without my things.
Lost and found:	Of course we will. You can be sure of that, Mr Rodríguez. Goodbye.
Carlos Rodríguez:	Goodbye.

Task 2

Decide if the following sentences are true (T) or false (F).

1 The Reliance Mail Order Company are sure Mr Bronson hasn't paid.   T/F
2 Mr Bronson will check what has happened.   T/F
3 Mr Rodríguez' flight should have arrived at 8 o'clock.   T/F
4 His luggage has been lost before.   T/F
5 His number is 691273.   T/F

What to say – what to expect

HANDLING COMPLAINTS

Person called
Your complaint is perfectly justified, but may I explain the matter from our point of view?
Yes, I do understand your question. It's not easy for me to answer it right now, but I'll certainly try.
You see, when you asked us to make immediate delivery, we did all we could to meet your request.

ESTABLISHING A GOOD COMPANY IMAGE

Person called
Hello, can I help you?
Yes, there does seem to have been a mistake at our end. Thanks for telling me about it.
Something has obviously gone wrong. Please excuse us for this mistake.
It might be an advantage for you if Mr Roberts called on you.

Task 3

Choose the missing words from the box.

1 I have to phone you because your payment is ....
2 If you let us have fuller ...., we can .... out the question.
3 It's really a ...., arriving here without my luggage.
4 I can do .... about it if you can provide me with some more ....
5 And will I have to fill in and sign a .... or a ....?
6 Let me see if I've got the .... check number?
7 In the evening I can be .... at my hotel.
8 If I'm not there, please .... a message for me.

baggage	declaration	details	form	information	leave
nuisance	overdue	reached	something	sort	

Task 4

Choose the best responses.

1 I think there's been a slip somewhere.
    a What message?
    b Where's the note now?
    c What sort of mistake?

2 There may have been a mistake at our end.
    a So you've found it at last.
    b I don't know when the mistake was made.
    c Well, it certainly wasn't my fault.

3 I hope you can sort it out.
    a It's difficult to arrange.
    b I'm sure we'll find out what went wrong.
    c What sort do you want?

4 My luggage is missing. It's a damned nuisance.
    a I'm sorry it's giving you problems.
    b So you have a lot of cases?
    c We don't have any here.

5 If you give me the check number, we'll trace your baggage for you.
    a It's already labelled.
    b I don't need a duplicate number.
    c It's FL 052273.

6 I'm sure your complaint is justified.
    a I'm glad you've done it.
    b Yes, I've just made it.
    c It's not the first time either.

Task 5 🔲

Listen to the two telephone conversations on the cassette. While you are listening, complete the table below.

Call	Caller	Company called	Reason for call	Action
1				
2				

You will find the tapescript on pages 102–103.

What to say – what to expect

HANDLING COMPLAINTS

Person called
Yes, that's right up to a point, but this is how we see the situation.
We did our best to help you, but I do understand your point of view.
I'll tell you what I'll do. I'll find out as much as I can and ring you back this afternoon.

POSITIVELY-ORIENTED QUESTIONS

Person calling/Person called
Have you thought of this possibility?
Would you be interested in hearing our point of view?
May I make a few suggestions?
What do you think of this idea?
Can we come and give you a demonstration?
Is it feasible to coordinate our activities in this area?

Task 6 🔲

Listen to the telephone conversations on the cassette. While you are listening, complete the table below.

Call	Called person	Reason for call	Action/Weald	Action/other Co.
1				
2				

You will find the tapescript on pages 103–104.

Task 7 🔈

Listening check

1 What does Herr Lang offer to do?
2 What does Mr Kumar suggest?
3 What action will Herr Lang take?
4 How does Herr Lang apologise?
5 What does he think should happen to the faulty tents?
6 How much did Weald claim from the insurance company and how much did they originally get?
7 What was the reason for the difference?
8 What will the insurance company send them?

Task 8

Complete the following conversation with phrases from the list below.

Zeller Pharma.
  1 ....
A little. How can I help you?
  2 ....
Yes, that's correct. Who would you like to speak to?
  3 ....
Hold the line, please.
  4 ....
Good morning. This is Clive Brooking of Pharmarketing Ltd, London.
  5 ....
As I'm sure you know, we're doing some work on your new anti-histamine preparation.
  6 ....
And I made a preliminary arrangement to meet Mr Duensing this Friday.
  7 ....
And I wanted to confirm it.
  8 ....
What's the problem?
  9 ....
Oh, that's a real nuisance.
10 ....

a I'm very sorry for any inconvenience this causes you. Perhaps . . .
b Oh dear. I'm awfully sorry, Mr Brooking. It won't be possible.
c Yes, Herr Duensing said he was using a London consultancy.
d Do you speak English?
e That is Zeller Pharmaceuticals, isn't it?
f I see.
g Mr Duensing, please.
h Good morning, Mr Brooking.
i Herr Duensing's telephone. Anna Schmidt.
j Herr Duensing had to leave for New York suddenly yesterday.

LANGUAGE STUDY

Task 9   Fault diagnosis

When we are talking about faults, we use *may/might/could* to list the possible reasons; *should/ought to* to talk about what we expect to happen; *can't* to exclude various reasons; and *must* when we decide what the reason for the fault is. Look at the example below.

I can't get a dialling tone on my phone. It *may* be because there is a fault in the phone, or it *could* be in British Telecom's equipment, or I *might* not have plugged the phone in. So I check the plug. It's in the socket. So it *can't* be that. British Telecom say their equipment is OK. The phone *ought to* work, but it doesn't. The fault *must* be somewhere in the phone itself.

Now complete the fault diagnosis below.

My car doesn't start one morning. Why not? There are a number of possible explanations. It (1) .... be the battery. It (2) .... be the plugs. So I check them. Both of them are OK, so the car (3) .... start. But it doesn't. I put in a new starter motor last week so it (4) .... be that. Then I notice that the needle in the petrol gauge is pointing at zero. It (5) .... be the petrol. The tank (6) .... be empty. If I put some petrol in, it (7) .... start. The petrol gauge (8) .... be faulty, but I don't think it is.

Task 10   Nouns and verbs

Noun	Verb	Noun	Verb
1	announce	9 description	....
2 schedule	....	10 preparation	....
3 lunch	....	11	delay
4	apologise	12 arrival	....
5	prefer	13	recommend
6 statement	....	14 pleasure	....
7	complain	15 transmission	....
8	refer	16	depart

SPEAKING

Task 11 [cassette]

Listen to the callers on the cassette. They will ask you for the information which is given below.

1 ASAP	6 009 33 62 817154
2 Abu Dhabi	7 Harjeet Singh Lal
3 9·615 tons	8 ETA 11.45 a.m.
4 13 April	9 £175 − 10% = £157.50
5 D-7000	10 Llanrwst

Task 12 [cassette]

Apologise to and help these callers. You may listen to the conversations on cassette first to help you.

Task 13   Role play

Do this exercise in pairs. Student B has information below, student A on page 107.

B1 You work in a post office in the USA. The information below will help you to answer a foreign caller's questions.

Letters to Europe			
Weight (grammes)	up to 20	21 – 40	41 – 100
Surface	20c	35c	50c
Air	45c	85c	$1.40

Insurance (both surface and air) is 40c per 15 grammes.
Delivery: 2 to 4 days (air) 8 to 12 days (surface).

B2 You work in a travel agency in the USA. The information below will help you to change a foreign visitor's airline booking.

Flights from MIAMI to NEW YORK (every afternoon)				
Flight no.	Airline	dep	arr	notes
EA 612	Eastern	13.00	15.00	
FA 326/491	Air Florida	14.00	17.30	change in New Orleans
EA 614	Eastern	15.00	17.00	fully booked
FA 792/442	Air Florida	16.15	19.30	change in Atlanta, Georgia
FA 806	Air Florida	17.15	19.15	

B3 You are Joanne Spencer in New York. You will be out of town on 18 May, but your assistant, Mark Bauer, is available.

TELECOM SERVICES

Task 14

Read the description of Prestel below and then choose an explanation for each of the special Prestel terms.

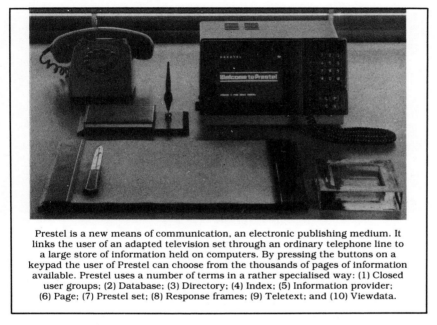

Prestel is a new means of communication, an electronic publishing medium. It links the user of an adapted television set through an ordinary telephone line to a large store of information held on computers. By pressing the buttons on a keypad the user of Prestel can choose from the thousands of pages of information available. Prestel uses a number of terms in a rather specialised way: (1) Closed user groups; (2) Database; (3) Directory; (4) Index; (5) Information provider; (6) Page; (7) Prestel set; (8) Response frames; (9) Teletext; and (10) Viewdata.

a These allow the user to communicate with the information provider.
b This is a guide to using Prestel which contains the official British Telecom indexes, and information and articles about the service.
c Teletext systems are different from viewdata systems like Prestel in that they broadcast their pages of information and do not use the telephone network.
d These are pages restricted to certain users.
e This is a rather specialised computing term used to describe the total amount of information used by the system. It is held in a number of large computers.
f A system for getting necessary information from a database using a modified television set.
g A television set with a keypad and equipment that is used to connect it to a telephone line.
h A display of information.
i A company or institution that makes information available, with or without cost, for viewdata users.
j The list of information and information providers the system covers.

LISTENING TRANSCRIPTS

UNIT 1

Task 5

GETTING INFORMATION

Ron Benson:	213562, Ron Benson.
Tom Parker:	Hello, Ron. Tom Parker here. How are you?
Ron Benson:	Oh, hello Tom. I'm fine. Er . . . rather busy at the moment . . .
Tom Parker:	Sorry to disturb you. I'll keep it short. Could you give me the address of that person you mentioned last week? You know, the woman who's got that import/export office in Manila.
Ron Benson:	Ah, you mean Maria Edwardes. Now let me see. Umm . . . I don't know her address offhand, but I can easily look it up for you. Or, Tom, I've got a better idea. Let me ring you back in about an hour. Are you at the office now?
Tom Parker:	Yes, I'll be here till about five thirty. Thanks a lot.
Ron Benson:	OK. You'll be hearing from me. So long. Bye now.

CHANGING ARRANGEMENTS

Operator:	Garston Motors Limited. Good morning.
Chris Ingersoll:	Good morning. IBD Industries here. I'd like to speak to someone about an order.
Operator:	Is it for motors, caller, or for parts?
Chris Ingersoll:	Both, actually.
Operator:	I see. I'll put you through to Mr Datta.
Chris Ingersoll:	Thank you.
Mr Datta:	Datta speaking.
Chris Ingersoll:	IBD Industries, Chris Ingersoll here. Morning, Mr Datta. Er . . . can I ask you to put forward our order?
Mr Datta:	Well, we'll see. What's the order number, please?
Chris Ingersoll:	Er . . . d'you mean . . .?
Mr Datta:	It's on the order acknowledgement we sent to you. It's probably a serial number starting MU and so on.
Chris Ingersoll:	Ah . . . yes, I've got it. Er . . . MU/3721.
Mr Datta:	Right. You ordered two KS pump motors and a series of spare parts.
Chris Ingersoll:	That's it. Could . . . could you possibly put forward delivery to next month? We need them sooner than we thought.
Mr Datta:	Next month. And . . . umm . . . you originally specified delivery at the end of May. I'll see what we can do. Can I ring you back, Mr Ingersoll?
Chris Ingersoll:	Yes, I'd be very glad if you would. Er . . . we thought May would be OK, but we've been given shorter deadlines ourselves. We'd very much like to have the order in April if at all possible.
Mr Datta:	Right. Could you give me your phone number? Or is it the one on the order?
Chris Ingersoll:	Yes, that's the number. Let me give you my extension too. It's 319. Chris Ingersoll.
Mr Datta:	OK. You'll be hearing from me. I'll give you a call this afternoon.

| Chris Ingersoll: | Ah, that's fine. Thanks very much. Goodbye. |
| Mr Datta: | Goodbye. |

Task 7

RON BENSON RINGS BACK

Tom Parker:	703129. Parker speaking.
Ron Benson:	Is that you, Tom. It's Ron. I said I'd phone you back.
Tom Parker:	Ah, Ron. Sorry I disturbed you before.
Ron Benson:	Oh, that's OK. You couldn't have known that I had someone here then. Listen, you wanted Maria Edwardes' address, didn't you?
Tom Parker:	Yes, have you got it?
Ron Benson:	Mm, here it is. Miss Maria Edwardes – Edwardes spelt E-D-W-A-R-D-E-S, 18 Dones Street, Cavite City, Manila.
Tom Parker:	Thanks a lot. May I just repeat it? Maria Edwardes, Edwardes with an E at the end, 80 Dones Street, Cavite …
Ron Benson:	No, it's eighteen, not eighty.
Tom Parker:	OK, 18 Dones Street, Cavite City, Manila. Well, thanks again. Sorry to have troubled you.
Ron Benson:	Not at all. You're welcome. Hope to see you again soon. Bye then, Tom.
Tom Parker:	Bye Ron. Take care.

MR DATTA RINGS BACK

Operator:	IBD Industries.
Mr Datta:	Could I have extension 319, please?
Operator:	Extension 319. The phone's ringing … I'm sorry, caller, there's no reply.
Mr Datta:	Oh … I wanted to speak to Mr Ingersoll. When will he be in?
Operator:	Well, he should be in the building. Would you hold on, please. I'll try and get him on the bleeper.
Mr Ingersoll:	Hello, Ingersoll speaking.
Mr Datta:	Hello, this is Mr Datta. I'm phoning back about your order for the two KS pumps and parts.
Mr Ingersoll:	Oh yes, good, What's the situation? Can you do anything?
Mr Datta:	Yes, I've checked with the plant. We can send you the whole lot by the 20th of April.
Mr Ingersoll:	Ah, that's great, really great! Thanks very much. Can I really count on it?
Mr Datta:	We've rescheduled your order so that we can get it assembled by the middle of April. Then we can dispatch it before the twentieth.
Mr Ingersoll:	I'm very pleased about that. And I'm very grateful to you for arranging things.
Mr Datta:	Er … that's all right. We're always glad to help if we can. I'll telex the new arrangements to you.
Mr Ingersoll:	Good, and once again, many thanks. Bye bye.
Mr Datta:	Bye then.

UNIT 2

Task 5

WRONG NUMBER

Peter Wilson:	Hello, Peter Wilson here. Can I speak to Mr Hewitt?
Operator:	Sorry, there's no Mr Hewitt at this number.
Peter Wilson:	The number I have here is Packard Enterprises – Butler 34992.

Operator:	That's our number all right, but this is Packard Electric. You must have the wrong Packard from the phone book.
Peter Wilson:	Sorry. I'll take another look in the yellow pages.
Operator:	That's all right. Bye.
Peter Wilson:	Bye.

MAKING AND CONFIRMING ARRANGEMENTS

Bob Troy:	Hello, can you give me Jack Nelson, please?
Secretary:	Hold on please. I'll see if he's in his office.
Jack Nelson:	Nelson here. What can I do for you?
Bob Troy:	Hello Jack. Bob Troy from Dominion Light.
Jack Nelson:	Hi Bob, good to hear from you. What's on your mind?
Bob Troy:	Jack, we talked about getting together to discuss the spring sales meeting. I'm going to be in your area next Wednesday. What about getting together then?
Jack Nelson:	That sounds fine, Bob. Why don't we have lunch together at Hardings?
Bob Troy:	Good idea. Shall we say 12.30 at the bar?
Jack Nelson:	That's fine with me, Bob.
Bob Troy:	See you on Wednesday, then. Bye.
Jack Nelson:	Bye.

Task 6

WEALD PLC OF WATFORD, ENGLAND, ARE IMPORTERS AND WHOLESALERS FOR SPORTS AND CAMPING EQUIPMENT. THEIR BELGIAN SUPPLIER CONTACTS THEM

André Max:	Good afternoon, Maxton Company of Brussels here. May I speak to Pat Thompson, please?
Operator:	Yes, he's in. I'll just put you through. Who's calling, please?
André Max:	André Max here.
Operator:	Pat, Mr Max is phoning from Brussels. Shall I put him through?
Pat Thompson:	Oh, good. Yes, do. . . . Pat Thompson speaking.
André Max:	Oh, hello Pat. How are things?
Pat Thompson:	Well, busy you know. What about you? Any problems?
André Max:	No, not really. I just wanted to tell you about that consignment you're waiting for.
Pat Thompson:	Ah yes, the surfboards. Good. You know, we're rather waiting for those.
André Max:	Mm, that's why I'm phoning. Here's the position. They've left our factory and are on their way to you. They're in two containers.
Pat Thompson:	Fine, then they'll be here on time.
André Max:	Yes, bound to be. And one of the containers also has the nylon sail material you ordered.
Pat Thompson:	Well, I'm glad to hear that. The documents are on the way, I suppose.
André Max:	Yes, of course. Well, that's what I wanted to talk to you about. Will you be coming over here soon?
Pat Thompson:	No, it doesn't look as though I'll be able to leave the office for the next month or two. Thanks very much for ringing, André.
André Max:	That's OK. Bye for now Pat.

WEALD PLC CALL A CUSTOMER

Operator:	Southern Sailing Club. Can I help you?
Pat Thompson:	Hello, Weald of Watford here. Who deals with surfboards and sails at your club?
Operator:	Buying, d'you mean? That's Cathy Lester. Shall I connect you?
Pat Thompson:	Please, if you would.

Cathy Lester:	Cathy Lester speaking.
Pat Thompson:	Hello, Thompson of Weald here. Was it you who ordered eight surfboards from us last month?
Cathy Lester:	Yes, I did. Any chance of getting them soon, Mr Thompson?
Pat Thompson:	Yes. I've got good news for you. They'll soon be on the way. We can dispatch them on Tuesday – that's the 16th.
Cathy Lester:	Oh good. They'll be here in time for our instructor to check everything...

UNIT 3

Task 5

ASKING ABOUT TICKETS

Booking Clerk:	Concert Bookings, good morning.
Jack Snow:	This is Jack Snow. Can you tell me if there are any tickets left for the Boston Symphony Orchestra on Sunday?
Booking Clerk:	Sorry, the concert is completely sold out. You might try the box office just before the performance. We often have last minute cancellations.
Jack Snow:	How much are the tickets?
Booking Clerk:	It's a unit price of ten dollars a ticket.
Jack Snow:	All right then. Thanks very much. Bye.
Booking Clerk:	Bye now.

TRYING TO GET THE BEST PRICE ON A NEW CAR

Customer:	Hello, Ed Reilly speaking. I'd like some information on the new Cutlass Supreme.
Secretary:	Er ... hang on, please. I'll connect you with one of our salesmen.
Salesman:	Sam Rizzo here, what can I do for you?
Customer:	Hello, er ... this is Ed Reilly. I'm looking for some information on the new Cutlass Supreme.
Salesman:	Fine, what would you like to know?
Customer:	Er ... first, ... has the new model already arrived?
Salesman:	Yes, we've got one on display in our showroom now.
Customer:	Are you running any special discounts on early purchases?
Salesman:	We might be able to do something for you, Ed.
Customer:	What kind of trade-ins are you offering on two-year-old models?
Salesman:	That's a difficult question to answer, Ed. Why don't you come down here? We can have a look at the new model and see how much we can give you on your old car.
Customer:	Er ... OK. I'll drop in tonight after work.
Salesman:	Terrific, see you then, Ed.
Customer:	Bye.

Task 6

WEALD PLC MAKES A PRICE INQUIRY

Operator:	Dugardin Compagnie, 'allo.
Pat Thompson:	Weald of Watford here. Good afternoon. Could you put me through to Mr Gilbert in sales, please?
Operator:	*Ne quittez pas...*
Luc Gilbert:	Gilbert speaking.

Pat Thompson:	Pat Thompson here. How are you Mr Gilbert?
Luc Gilbert:	Oh, fine, fine. Quite busy, actually.
Pat Thompson:	Well, I shouldn't complain about that. Look, I need the price of your model XT 12 and PT 20 tents.
Luc Gilbert:	OK, I've got them right here. Would it be for about a hundred?
Pat Thompson:	That's right. That price will do.
Luc Gilbert:	Here we are then: the XT 12 is 610 francs now ... but that's not a lot more than you paid last year, and the PT 20 is 774 francs. That's ex-works, of course.
Pat Thompson:	Right, I've got that: 610 francs for the XT 12 and 774 for the PT 20. Are they just the same as the ones we had last year?
Luc Gilbert:	The models are the same but we've got a couple of new colours for the smaller tent. Shall I send you some sample cuttings?
Pat Thompson:	Yes, if you would. Listen, Mr Gilbert, I'm not quite ready to place an order yet, but you'll be hearing from us soon. I really just wanted to check on the prices.
Luc Gilbert:	That's OK. But don't wait too long, will you? This month and next is our busy season and the demand's likely to be quite heavy. Our tents are such good value, as you know.
Pat Thompson:	All right, I'll let you know as soon as I can. Goodbye for now.
Luc Gilbert:	Goodbye, Mr Thompson. Thanks for calling.

AN INQUIRY ABOUT FOOTBALLS

Operator:	Weald of Watford. Can I help you?
Jim Hampton:	Yes, hello. This is Jim Hampton, buyer for Blacktons. I'm phoning for some prices for footballs.
Operator:	Right, I'll put you on to our sales office. Just a moment, please. I have a Mr Jim Hampton from Blacktons on the line. Can you take it, Mr Dawson?
Mr Dawson:	Yes, put him through, would you? Dawson, Sales Department.
Jim Hampton:	Hello, Mr Dawson. We may be needing another fifty footballs from you. It's the leather hand-sewn ones we'd like. Can you give me a good price for them?
Mr Dawson:	Quality A Super. Yes, they're the best. For fifty that'd be £9.20 each.
Jim Hampton:	Oh, come now. I know that's what the price list says, but surely you can quote me better terms than that. What about a good discount? It's not our first order, you know.
Mr Dawson:	Yes, of course. You had a hundred earlier this year, didn't you? Well, I can give you the quantity discount that we allow for 200 or over. That's 7%. How does that sound?
Jim Hampton:	Couldn't you make it 10%? We must be one of your best customers.
Mr Dawson:	Tell you what. 7%'s the most I can do in the way of a quantity discount, but there's another 2% for payment within ten days. How's that?
Jim Hampton:	All right. I think I can order on those terms. I'll put it in the mail to you. I'd rather give it to you in writing.
Mr Dawson:	Right, and we'll send off the footballs immediately from stock.
Jim Hampton:	That's fine. Goodbye then.
Mr Dawson:	Goodbye, Mr Hampton.

UNIT 4

Task 5

ORDERING FLOWERS

Saleswoman:	Hello. Worldwide Flowers. Mrs Green speaking.
Jim Kelly:	This is Jim Kelly. I'd like to order some flowers and have them sent to my home.
Saleswoman:	Fine, Mr Kelly. What kind of flowers did you have in mind?
Jim Kelly:	I'd like to send a dozen red roses.
Saleswoman:	A dozen red roses. Our long-stem red roses are selling for twelve dollars a dozen this week, and they're really quite nice.
Jim Kelly:	All right then. I'll take those.
Saleswoman:	I'll need your complete address with the zip code, Mr Kelly.
Jim Kelly:	The address is: 43 Pennsylvania Avenue, Bloomington, Indiana, 47401.
Saleswoman:	What would you like us to put on the card?
Jim Kelly:	Hm, just something simple. How about: All my love, Jim.
Saleswoman:	OK. Now, when should they arrive?
Jim Kelly:	They should be there before six in the evening on September the 12th.
Saleswoman:	That should be no problem. Just one more question, Mr Kelly. How do you intend to make payment?
Jim Kelly:	You can put it on my Visa card. The number is: JK 409.6237.
Saleswoman:	That should do it. Thank you for calling Worldwide Flowers. Bye.
Jim Kelly:	Bye.

ORDERING WINE

Distributor:	Western Liquor Distribution. Good morning.
Bill Patterson:	Hello, this is Bill Patterson of Patterson's Liquor in Albany. I'm interested in increasing my selection of red wines. Have you got any new California reds on stock?
Distributor:	Can you hold the line for a minute, Mr Patterson? I'll connect you with Dennis Murphy, our wine specialist.
Dennis Murphy:	Hello, Dennis Murphy speaking. Can I help you?
Bill Patterson:	Yes, Dennis. This is Bill Patterson of Patterson's Liquor in Albany. I think we talked once before.
Dennis Murphy:	Ah yes, Mr Patterson. I remember now. What can I do for you?
Bill Patterson:	This is my question. Several of my customers have expressed interest in the full-bodied California red wines they have had in other parts of the country. Do you have any at the present time?
Dennis Murphy:	Yes, as a matter of fact, I've got the new products from Nappa Valley that are very popular at the moment. I could send you a few cases of each on a trial basis.
Bill Patterson:	That sounds fine. I'll need them as soon as possible.
Dennis Murphy:	Good. I can see to it that you have them by the end of the week. We've got your address, haven't we?
Bill Patterson:	Yes, you have.
Dennis Murphy:	Will there be anything else?
Bill Patterson:	No, I think that's it for now.
Dennis Murphy:	All right, bye now.
Bill Patterson:	Bye.

Task 6

Mr Gilbert:	*M. Gilbert à l'appareil.*
Pat Thompson:	Hello, Mr Gilbert. This is Pat Thompson of Weald in England.
Mr Gilbert:	Hello, Mr Thompson. What can I do for you?
Pat Thompson:	You know the quote you gave me for a hundred XT 12 tents about a week ago...?
Mr Gilbert:	Yes, the lightweight ones. I remember.
Pat Thompson:	Well, we'd like to order a thousand.
Mr Gilbert:	A thousand. Just a minute please and I'll check. Yes, that's no problem. We can dispatch them almost immediately. We'll send them to London Heathrow by air freight, shall we? You'd have them by about the 20th.
Pat Thompson:	That's wonderful. I'd just like to confirm the price. It was 610 francs, wasn't it?
Mr Gilbert:	That's it.
Pat Thompson:	But for a thousand – could you make a little concession? Your quotation was for a hundred.
Mr Gilbert:	Now, let's see. A thousand – yes. We could make it 560 francs net for payment by draft on our bank or by cheque to us direct. Actually I'd prefer the latter in view of the rush.
Pat Thompson:	That's OK. I'll get that in the mail today.
Mr Gilbert:	Fine, then I'll get things moving here and we'll dispatch the consignment as soon as I get your payment. Anything else I can do for you?
Pat Thompson:	Not just at the moment. I'll be in touch with you when there is.
Mr Gilbert:	OK. Thanks for ringing, Mr Thompson. I'll take good care of your order. Bye.

Operator:	Weald of Watford. Good morning.
James McPherson:	McPhersons of Edinburgh here. Is that the Sales Department?
Operator:	Hold on, please. I'll connect you.
Harry Dawson:	Sales Department, Harry Dawson speaking.
James McPherson:	James McPherson of Edinburgh. Mr Dawson, I'd like to come straight to the point. We've had a rush on tennis shoes this season and we need some more in a hurry.
Harry Dawson:	I expect we can supply them. Could you tell me what kind you'd like and give me an idea of the quantity? You've got our price list, I suppose?
James McPherson:	Yes, I have. We had your 'Tournament' line, but the 'Champion' shoes that are in your price list might do as well. As far as ... er ... quantities are concerned, we would like 50 pairs in each of the most usual sizes and about 30 in sizes 35 and 45.
Harry Dawson:	Yes, Mr McPherson. That's for immediate delivery, is it?
James McPherson:	The sooner you can send them, the better.
Harry Dawson:	Hm, let's see. I can do the 'Champion' shoes in the numbers and sizes you want. We haven't got enough 'Tournament' in some of the sizes, though.
James McPherson:	Umm...that's too bad. They were very popular with our customers.
Harry Dawson:	Yes, we've noticed that all over the country. We've got some more on order, actually, but we can't supply them until the beginning of August.
James McPherson:	No, that's too late. OK, would you send us the 'Champion' line. I'll put my order in the mail to you.
Harry Dawson:	Well, Mr McPherson, thanks; but it'd save time if I noted your order now. Could you just repeat the number you need...

UNIT 5

Task 5

MAKING TRAVEL ARRANGEMENTS

Operator:	Continental Express. Good afternoon.
Elaine Morrison:	Good afternoon. John Hill, please.
Operator:	Who's calling, please?
Elaine Morrison:	Elaine Morrison.
Operator:	I'll connect you.
Elaine Morrison:	Thank you.
John Hill:	John Hill.
Elaine Morrison:	Hello, John. How are you?
John Hill:	Elaine! Good to hear from you. How are things?
Elaine Morrison:	Fine thanks. And how are you?
John Hill:	Oh, fine.
Elaine Morrison:	Good. Now I know you're going to be thrilled. I finally have my vacation plans pinned down, and I would like to make some reservations.
John Hill:	Well, Elaine, I'll be glad to help you. What have you decided?
Elaine Morrison:	I'm going to Boston and Hyannas.
John Hill:	Sounds good. What dates are you travelling on?
Elaine Morrison:	Er ... starting Monday, July 26. About midday – late morning or early afternoon.
John Hill:	Let me just check. Hang on for a moment, please. You still there, Elaine? I can get you on a noon flight from Kennedy to Boston. How does that sound?
Elaine Morrison:	That's just fine.
John Hill:	OK. Now, where are you planning to stay?
Elaine Morrison:	Moving right along here, John – Ritz Carlton Hotel, Boston. Would you make reservations for Monday, July 26 and Tuesday, July 27. Two nights, single with bath, please.
John Hill:	July 26 and 27, single with bath. Yes, I've noted that.
Elaine Morrison:	Yes, fine. Now, Wednesday, July 28 ... an a.m. flight Boston to Hyannas. Can you do that for me?
John Hill:	Just have a look. Hey, Elaine, I've got just what you want. Departure from Boston at 10.45. How's that?
Elaine Morrison:	Fine – terrific. Can I pick up the tickets this evening?
John Hill:	Of course. And I hope there'll be time for us to have a drink together.
Elaine Morrison:	That'd be great. See you later, John. Thanks.

CANCELLING A HOTEL BOOKING

Hotel:	Excelsior Hotel.
Caller:	Hello, I'm ringing from the university. I made a reservation for the 14th, and um ... now I'm afraid I shall have to cancel it.
Hotel:	Just a moment, please, caller, I'll put you on to Advance Reservations.
Clerk:	Advance Reservations, can I help you?
Caller:	Yes, I'm phoning up because I booked a room for an overseas visitor who won't be able to come now and so I'll have to cancel it, I'm afraid.
Clerk:	What name is it, please, and when was it for?
Caller:	It was a double room booked in the name of Dr R. Siddhu from the 14th for a week.
Clerk:	Ah yes, I've got it, from the 14th to the 20th September. And now you want to change the booking, do you?
Caller:	I wish I could, but it now appears that he won't be able to come at all.
Clerk:	Well, madam, I'll cancel it then. I hope we can help you at some other time.

Task 6

Pat Thompson: Pat Thompson of Weald, Watford, England here. Is Mr Bengtsson in this afternoon?

Operator: Yes, I believe so. Sorry, I didn't catch your name.

Pat Thompson: My name is Pat Thompson and I'm calling from Weald in England.

Operator: Thank you, Mr Thompson. I'll put you through to Mr Bengtsson now.

Mr Bengtsson: Bengtsson.

Pat Thompson: Mr Bengtsson, hello. Pat Thompson of Weald here. Thanks for your letter of the 29th March. I got it today and I'm phoning to save time.

Mr Bengtsson: Ah yes, thanks. So, is it all right if I come to your place next week?

Pat Thompson: It certainly is. We're very glad you could arrange it for the 10th. Our Managing Director, Wesley Weald, is looking forward to seeing you this time, too. And I feel that a personal discussion is best if we want to work out the terms of the contract satisfactorily.

Mr Bengtsson: Quite right. It's so much simpler than lots of letters.

Pat Thompson: Now, Mr Bengtsson, tell me. Shall we make a hotel reservation for you?

Mr Bengtsson: Well, yes, that might be an idea. I was really wondering whether to stay in London or in Watford.

Pat Thompson: Well, we're very much hoping you'll be our guest at dinner on Monday evening...

Mr Bengtsson: That's very kind of you.

Pat Thompson: ...so it may be convenient for you to stay locally, at the King's Head Hotel, say. It's a good hotel, not too luxurious but quite comfortable.

Mr Bengtsson: Yes, that sounds fine. Would you arrange for them to put me up on Sunday and Monday night, then?

Pat Thompson: OK, I'll see to that. Sunday the 9th and Monday the 10th.

Mr Bengtsson: Could you let me have the phone number of the hotel?

Pat Thompson: Yes, hang on a second. Here it is ... 0923 7372218.

Mr Bengtsson: Right ... 0923 7372218. Is it easy to find?

Pat Thompson: If you're coming from London, there's a very good train service to Watford and the hotel's just round the corner from the station, at 2 Harrow Road. And if you're flying to Heathrow, it would be simplest to take a taxi. It's not too far.

Mr Bengtsson: That's what I'll do then. Now let me see. You're expecting me at 11 o'clock, aren't you?

Pat Thompson: Yes, if that suits you. Look, I'll tell you what I'll do. If you're staying at the King's Head Hotel, shall I come and fetch you at, say, a quarter to eleven, and bring you to our offices?

Mr Bengtsson: Well, if you would.

Pat Thompson: Fine, that's fixed then. Is there anything else you might need?

Mr Bengtsson: No, I don't think so. You're very helpful, Mr Thompson.

Pat Thompson: Not at all. Well, I hope you have a good trip.

Mr Bengtsson: Thanks a lot. See you on the 10th, then. Goodbye now.

Pat Thompson: Yes, be seeing you soon. Bye now.

Matthew Sharp: Hello, Pat, Matthew Sharp here.

Pat Thompson: Hello, Matthew. How are you doing?

Matthew Sharp: Could be better at this end, Pat, I can tell you. How are things with you?

Pat Thompson: Not so bad. What's the problem, then?

Matthew Sharp: Well, you know that new customer you wanted me to call on in Barry – the Evanson Company. I must have spent half a day searching around and then I didn't get hold of them.

Pat Thompson:	How come?
Matthew Sharp:	They've moved twice and now they've gone broke.
Pat Thompson:	Oh hell, they owe us quite a lot. A thousand at least.
Matthew Sharp:	Yes, and we're not the only ones. But what I really wanted to tell you is this: I'm going up north now and as my itinerary has changed, I wanted to let you know where you can contact me until the weekend.
Pat Thompson:	OK, I'm ready.
Matthew Sharp:	Tomorrow I'll be in Ebbw Vale, where I'll be visiting Ashton and Taylor. Then Newton on Thursday and then on to Welshpool.
Pat Thompson:	So you'll be in Welshpool on Friday, will you?
Matthew Sharp:	No, I can manage both of those in one day. You could contact me in Wrexham on Friday. I'll book into the Welsh Harp Hotel on Thursday evening. That's where I usually stay. You can leave a message if you like.
Pat Thompson:	Right. But would you give me another call beforehand, say on Thursday in the late morning? We're having a sales meeting, and I'm sure to have some news for you.
Matthew Sharp:	Yes, there was some talk about some new introductory offers, wasn't there?
Pat Thompson:	That's right. I'd like you to be in the picture when we've reached a decision on that.
Matthew Sharp:	Fine, then, you'll be hearing from me again on Thursday. Bye for now.
Pat Thompson:	Cheers then. Thanks for ringing.

UNIT 6

Task 5

ARRANGING FOR A SERVICE CHECK

Susan Johnson:	Hello, IBM Sales and Service, Susan Johnson speaking.
John Deluca:	Good morning Mrs Johnson, John Deluca of New York Life here.
Susan Johnson:	Oh . . . hello Mr Deluca, what can I do for you?
John Deluca:	We bought an IBM-X20 from you about six months ago and we're having some problems with it.
Susan Johnson:	Can you tell me what the main problem is, Mr Deluca?
John Deluca:	I don't think that it's anything major. It just seems that the quality of the printouts could be better.
Susan Johnson:	I see. Has your staff been given instruction on how to operate the machine?
John Deluca:	I don't believe we've had any formal instruction yet, Mrs Johnson.
Susan Johnson:	That's strange. I'll send a service operator over. If you'd like, he could also give your staff some instruction on how to use your new IBM-X20.
John Deluca:	That sounds fine.
Susan Johnson:	When would it be convenient for you?
John Deluca:	How about Wednesday at two in the afternoon?
Susan Johnson:	That would be possible. I'll send you a confirmation of that appointment.
John Deluca:	Thanks very much. Bye Mrs Johnson.
Susan Johnson:	Thanks for calling, Mr Deluca. Bye.

ARRANGING A JOB INTERVIEW

Cheryl Nelson:	Hello, could you connect me with the Personnel Department, please?
Operator:	Just a moment, please . . . Go ahead . . .
Frank Sharp:	Hello, Frank Sharp, Personnel.
Cheryl Nelson:	This is Cheryl Nelson speaking. I'm calling about the Administrative Assistant position you advertised in yesterday's *Daily Courier*.
Frank Sharp:	Ah yes, that job is still open, Miss Nelson. If you feel that you fulfil the qualifi-

cations listed, we could arrange for a job interview.

Cheryl Nelson:	Yes, Mr Sharp, I do have those qualifications and I am very interested in that job.
Frank Sharp:	Fine, Miss Nelson. When would it be convenient for you to come in for an interview?
Cheryl Nelson:	Any time next week Mr Sharp. Mornings are usually better for me.
Frank Sharp:	Umm . . . shall we say nine o'clock on Tuesday.
Cheryl Nelson:	Hang on, I'll check my appointment book . . . yes, that would suit me.
Frank Sharp:	OK. I'll see you on Tuesday at nine. Goodbye.
Cheryl Nelson:	Goodbye, Mr Sharp.

Task 6

WEALD ARE PLANNING A CONFERENCE

Pat Thompson:	Hello, Susan, how are you these days?
Susan Shields:	Hi, Pat! Nice to hear from you again.
Pat Thompson:	Look, Susan, I'm phoning you because we've got to put on a conference next month, and I remember you made most of the arrangements last time. And things went so smoothly, I thought I couldn't do better than ask you for some tips.
Susan Shields:	I'd be glad to help. Is it a sales conference again?
Pat Thompson:	Yes, in a way. It's mainly for agents, and we're inviting a few of our influential customers. The objectives are mainly to introduce the products we're putting on the market next season, to describe our services to customers, and so on.
Susan Shields:	And how many people are expected to attend this time? Last year it was about 120.
Pat Thompson:	Yes, We're counting on 150 this time. No more.
Susan Shields:	And is it during the school holidays? If so, you could use the Technical College again.
Pat Thompson:	That's the trouble. It'll be a bit later this year, so I was thinking of the Northwest Conference Hall. It's big enough, I think, though it'll be more expensive.
Susan Shields:	Yes, I remember. We went there about five years ago. But have they got enough rooms for discussion groups? I suppose there'll be some group meetings as well, or workshops.
Pat Thompson:	Well, I must go into that. We haven't worked out all those details yet. Then there are other things to arrange like loudspeakers and visual aids. I'm going to make a checklist.
Susan Shields:	Yes, I did that too. I say, Pat, have you got the files I had on last year's conference? They'd give you some help. And, of course I'd be glad to give you a hand too.
Pat Thompson:	That would be great, Susan. I'd very much like the chance of using some of your experience. May I invite you to lunch, and then we could have a bit of a planning session about it all afterwards. What about next Wednesday?
Susan Shields:	I think that's OK by me. I'll ring you back, shall I?
Pat Thompson:	Please do. Looking forward to hearing from you again, Susan, and thanks.
Susan Shields:	That's OK, Pat. Bye.

INVITING A SPEAKER

Jim Harris:	Harris speaking.
Pat Thompson:	Pat Thompson here, of Weald in Watford. Good afternoon, Mr Harris.
Jim Harris:	Afternoon.
Pat Thompson:	Mr Harris, I'm phoning to ask you whether you'd give a talk at our conference next month?
Jim Harris:	A talk? Well, I don't really know. Who did you say you were?

Pat Thompson:	We're Weald, manufacturers and wholesalers of sports equipment. You may know our 'Champion' and 'Tournament' tennis shoes, or maybe Weald surf-boards.
Jim Harris:	No, sorry, I'm not keen on sports. But what is it you're ringing me about?
Pat Thompson:	I heard you speak at a symposium on advertising in London about a year ago, Mr Harris, and as you're an authority on the subject, I wanted to ask you if you'd be prepared to come to a conference we're holding next month as guest speaker.
Jim Harris:	Oh, I see. Yes, I might. When is it, and what would you like me to deal with?
Pat Thompson:	Well, the subject of the conference is marketing and sales, and I was wondering if you could give us a talk – say fifty minutes or so – on cost-effective publicity. The dates are from the 20th to the 22nd September and you could choose the time that'd suit you best on the 20th or 21st. We would pay £200 plus expenses.
Jim Harris:	That sounds fine. The morning of the 21st of September would be the most convenient. And you'd like about an hour's talk. What about question time? Shall we allow about a quarter of an hour for that?
Pat Thompson:	That would be a possibility, but we're tending more towards discussion in small groups or workshops. We split the people into working groups so that they can go into the practical aspects of what's been said in the lectures and how it affects their own field of work.
Jim Harris:	Yes, that's a good way of working.
Pat Thompson:	Of course, if you'd like to stay until the afternoon, we could have a panel discussion and then...
Jim Harris:	Sorry, Mr Thompson, I'm booked up that afternoon.
Pat Thompson:	Oh, too bad. Will you need any visual aids, a slide projector...

UNIT 7

Task 5

A COMPLAINT FROM THE EXECUTIVE MANAGER OF INTERNATIONAL PAPER

Doug Saxton:	Hello, this is Doug Saxton of International Paper. I'd like to speak to the Office Manager.
Operator:	Hold the line, please, I'll see if Mrs Sullivan is in ... Go ahead, Mrs Sullivan can take your call.
Doug Saxton:	Hello, Mrs Sullivan, this is Doug Saxton of International Paper. I'm afraid I have to make a serious complaint.
May Sullivan:	Hello, Mr Saxton. What seems to be the trouble?
Doug Saxton:	I've been flying Sun Air for nearly five years, Mrs Sullivan, and I must say that I have always been very satisfied with the service, but last Tuesday something happened which was inexcusable.
May Sullivan:	Can you give me the details, Mr Saxton?
Doug Saxton:	Yes. I was scheduled on Flight 401 from Washington to New York with a connecting flight out of New York to Boston the same morning. Your flight agent, Mr Green, assured me that I would have plenty of time to catch the plane to Boston. However, it was impossible to make that connection and, as a result, I was late for a very important business meeting.
May Sullivan:	I see. I'm very sorry to hear that, Mr Saxton. I can assure you that such things don't happen very often.
Doug Saxton:	I hope not. What do you intend to do about this, Mrs Sullivan?
May Sullivan:	I'll look into the matter for you, Mr Saxton, and talk to the person responsible for this mistake.
Doug Saxton:	All right, then.

May Sullivan:	Thanks for calling, Mr Saxton. If you have any further questions about exact flight schedules, don't hesitate to contact me direct.
Doug Saxton:	I'll do that, Mrs Sullivan. Goodbye.
May Sullivan:	Goodbye, Mr Saxton.

A MAIL-ORDER SHOPPING PROBLEM

Operator:	Hello, Brand Names Mail Order.
Jim Adams:	Would you connect me with the Customer Service Department, please?
Operator:	Just a moment, please.
Sam Jacobs:	Customer Service, Sam Jacobs here. Can I help you?
Jim Adams:	Yes, this is Jim Adams speaking. I'm afraid there's been a mix-up. I ordered a 3M tape recorder from you and I'm afraid someone has made a mistake and sent me the wrong model.
Sam Jacobs:	Ah ... I'm sorry about that, Mr Adams. Can you give me your order number and the exact catalogue number and description of the model you ordered?
Jim Adams:	Yes, let's see. I've got the bill right here. The order number is CS 124.39 and the model I ordered is the TR 3M-20 portable.
Sam Jacobs:	Thank you, Mr Adams. I'll have the correct recorder sent to you as soon as possible.
Jim Adams:	When can I expect delivery?
Sam Jacobs:	Umm ... you should have the 3M-20 by Friday at the latest. May I ask you to return the model you now have? We'll reimburse you for the postage, of course.
Jim Adams:	All right. I'll send the 3M-10 back.
Sam Jacobs:	I'm very sorry for the inconvenience, Mr Adams.
Jim Adams:	All right. I'm glad we can take care of the problem. Goodbye.
Sam Jacobs:	Goodbye, Mr Adams, and thanks for shopping Brand Names.

Task 6

WEALD HAVE AN ANGRY CUSTOMER ON THE LINE

Mr Tomlin:	Hello, Tomlin here. Put me on to your sales department, or maybe your dispatch department, would you?
Operator:	Yes, sir. May I ask who you're looking for or what it's about?
Mr Tomlin:	It's about your damn delivery! Those tennis shoes you sent me: most of them aren't even what I ordered.
Operator:	Well, it's our order processing office you'd be wanting. Just a minute, please, and I'll connect you.
Mr Graham:	Graham speaking.
Mr Tomlin:	Are you the person who deals with orders that have gone wrong?
Mr Graham:	Well, occasionally there's a problem with one of our orders and then it's likely to be me who deals with it. How can I help you?
Mr Tomlin:	Look, we've just received a consignment of tennis shoes. We've been waiting long enough for them and now, when they do finally arrive, we find they're the wrong ones.
Mr Graham:	I'm sorry to hear that. Could you tell me what your order number was?
Mr Tomlin:	My order number, or yours?
Mr Graham:	The number on our order acknowledgement, Mr Tomlin. It's in the top right-hand corner.
Mr Tomlin:	Let me just check. Ah, here it is: 0073921.
Mr Graham:	0073921. Right. And what exactly is wrong with the delivery?
Mr Tomlin:	One box is OK but the other two have different shoes from the ones we ordered. There aren't enough 'Champions' but there are too many 'Tournaments'. And they're nearly all the same size.

Mr Graham:	Yes, there's obviously been some mix-up, Mr Tomlin. I'll have to go into this with our warehouse, but I'll ring you back as soon as I can.
Mr Tomlin:	Look, I've got to know when that's going to be. And what about the shoes? Delays like this can have a really bad effect on my sales.
Mr Graham:	Yes, I realise that. But we've got plenty in stock and as soon as I've looked into things I'll be able to get the right ones off to you. You may even have them tomorrow.
Mr Tomlin:	Well, that'd certainly help. OK. I won't be in the office for the rest of the morning, so perhaps you could ring me back this afternoon, Mr Graham. Say about half past two.
Mr Graham:	Yes, I'll do that, Mr Tomlin. I'll be able to let you know the position. I'm very sorry you've been inconvenienced.
Mr Tomlin:	So am I. I'm busy enough without having to phone around for things like this.
Mr Graham:	I hope you'll believe this, Mr Tomlin, but it's something that doesn't often happen.
Mr Tomlin:	Well, I'll believe you. Thousands wouldn't. And you see that you can set things straight for me. Then I'll forgive and forget.
Mr Graham:	Of course I will. Goodbye for now.
Mr Tomlin:	Bye.

SETTING THINGS STRAIGHT

Mr Graham:	Morning, Fred, I've just had an angry customer on the line.
Fred Lucas:	That so? What was the problem?
Mr Graham:	It's job number 0073921. Can you look up the delivery note for it?
Fred Lucas:	Hang on. Er ... yes, here it is. A consignment for Tomlin Sport, in Warrington.
Mr Graham:	That's right. Now, what was sent to them? Was it three boxes?
Fred Lucas:	Yes, that's it. Now let me just compare the delivery note with the order. Oh hell, I can see what's gone wrong. I'm awfully sorry, Jim, the second page is for another customer.
Mr Graham:	What does that mean?
Fred Lucas:	It looks as if two boxes weren't correctly labelled. Tomlin Sport has got part of an order that should have gone to Warringtons Stores in Birmingham.
Mr Graham:	Ah ... so I can expect another panic phone call, then?
Fred Lucas:	Sorry about that.
Mr Graham:	Oh, well, these things can happen. Now how can we sort it all out? It'd take too long to have the Birmingham shoes redirected. The best solution would be to send Tomlin Sport the shoes they need from stock — I mean, there are plenty here — and ask them to redirect the wrong ones. That seems the best way to do it, doesn't it?
Fred Lucas:	Yes, I suppose so. Er ... I'll need another job card, though.
Mr Graham:	No problem. I'll make one out now and bring it down to you straight away. Can you get them on their way today?
Fred Lucas:	Yes, I'll manage that. Er ... but what about the Birmingham people. I'm not quite with you ...

UNIT 8

Task 5

A MISUNDERSTANDING

Sam Rizzo:	Bargain Rental, Sam Rizzo speaking.
Fred Barnes:	Hello, Mr Rizzo. This is Fred Barnes. I'm afraid there's been a mix-up and I'd like to clear the matter up as soon as possible.
Sam Rizzo:	What seems to be the problem, Mr Barnes?

Fred Barnes:	Let's see . . . two weeks ago I rented a small Ford economy car from your downtown office. The agent there told me that I could have that car for 20 dollars a day, mileage included. When my son returned the car last week, the agent insisted that he pay 20 dollars a day plus an additional charge of 20 cents a mile. My son paid the extra money, but I think that I should get the mileage money back.
Sam Rizzo:	I see. I think I know what the problem is, Mr Barnes. We don't offer the special mileage discount on our small economy cars.
Fred Barnes:	In that case your agent should have made that clear to me when I rented the car. I've been renting cars from Bargain Car Rental for years, Mr Rizzo, and this is no way to treat a regular customer.
Sam Rizzo:	I'm very sorry about that, Mr Barnes. You're right, the agent should have informed you the discount is limited to our middle-sized and luxury cars.
Fred Barnes:	Yes, I do believe it's the agent's fault.
Sam Rizzo:	I see no reason why you should have to pay for this mistake, Mr Barnes. If you send me the bill and your receipt of payment, I'll see to it that you get your money back.
Fred Barnes:	That's very kind of you, Mr Rizzo.
Sam Rizzo:	Don't mention it. Customer satisfaction is our main concern.
Fred Barnes:	Thanks again. Goodbye.
Sam Rizzo:	Goodbye, Mr Barnes.

IMPROVING THE COMPANY IMAGE

Mike Low:	Mike's Sporting Goods.
Ron Smith:	Hello, Mike. This is Ron Smith speaking.
Mike Low:	Hello, Ron. How are you? I haven't heard from you in ages.
Ron Smith:	I'm just fine, Mike.
Mike Low:	I'm glad to hear that, Ron. Now, what can I do for you?
Ron Smith:	Have you heard about our fund-raising project for young area athletes?
Mike Low:	I'm afraid I don't know anything about it yet, Ron.
Ron Smith:	Well, we're calling on all the local business people for a small contribution to help support our young athletes.
Mike Low:	Umm . . . how do you plan to use the money?
Ron Smith:	That's a good question, Mike. The money will be used to help finance team expenses at the state and regional meetings.
Mike Low:	That sounds like a good cause. It'll also be good advertising for our town.
Ron Smith:	That's right, Mike. Can we count on you for a small contribution?
Mike Low:	You sure can, Ron. I'll make out a check to you for one hundred dollars.
Ron Smith:	That's very generous, Mike. Your name and the name of your business will appear in next Saturday's *Evening News* under the list of major contributors.
Mike Low:	That's a pleasant surprise.
Ron Smith:	OK. Thanks again, Mike. Maybe I'll see you at the big game on Saturday?
Mike Low:	That's possible. Bye now, Ron.
Ron Smith:	Goodbye, Mike.

Task 6

FAULTY GOODS

Mr Kumar:	Weald Warehouse Control here. Can I speak to someone in your dispatch department, please? It's about your invoice C 139 022.
Operator:	Herr Lang is the person you want. Just a moment, please, and I'll connect you . . .
H Lang:	Lang speaking, Order Dispatch.
Mr Kumar:	Ah, hello, Mr Kumar here. From Weald of Watford.
H Lang:	Yes, hello, Mr Kumar. How can I help you?

Mr Kumar:	Well, I've got a bit of a problem here. You remember those tents we bought from you? Your invoice reference is C 139 022. Well, seven of them are absolutely useless, I'm afraid.
H Lang:	Oh, my word! What's wrong with them? They were in perfect condition when we sent them off.
Mr Kumar:	I don't know about that. There are five tents that have torn seams in almost the same place, just near the front opening, and another two where the tear has gone right into the side wall of the tent.
H Lang:	Is that so? How very strange, and in so many tents, too. I must say, your delivery was from a new consignment we had in about ... ooh ... six weeks ago. Er ... but our control system is usually very reliable.
Mr Kumar:	There seems to have been an oversight or something this time, though. I'm afraid we just can't accept these faulty goods.
H Lang:	Mr Kumar, could you give me a fuller description. Then I can investigate it for you.
Mr Kumar:	What, now, on the phone? I don't think that's a very good idea. No, I'll tell you what I can do. I'll have them photographed and send you the photos. In the meantime, would you make sure that we get replacements?
H Lang:	Ah ... that's a good idea, the photos. Yes, er, of course, we'll send replacements as soon as we can.
Mr Kumar:	Would you, please. We've got customers waiting for delivery.
H Lang:	In the meantime, I'd like to apologise on behalf of the company and thank you for being so cooperative about it.
Mr Kumar:	Well, if you get those new tents to us quickly, there's no great harm done. And will you let us know what to do with the faulty ones?
H Lang:	Yes. Can I get in touch with you again after we've had your photos? There may be some way we could have them repaired, or leave them with you at a reduced price.
Mr Kumar:	All right. I'll have them stored separately. How many photos ...

INSUFFICIENT PAYMENT

Mr Waters:	I'd like to talk to someone about your settlement slip DT3-19, dated 14 November.
Ms March:	Yes, that's right. We're the office for that. This is Christine March speaking.
Mr Waters:	And I'm Norman Waters of Weald in Watford. We put in a claim for damage in the amount of £420, and you've only paid us £369.60 as compensation. There's a kind of list attached, but I can't make out how on earth you've come to this amount.
Ms March:	Hold on a second and I'll get my copy. DT3-19, you said, didn't you?
Mr Waters:	That's right ...
Ms March:	Are you there, Mr Waters? Now let me see. The first item's the loss of that box of footballs from Pakistan, that's £220, and then there's ... oh, yes, you're right ... there's another item for £190 and claim expenses.
Mr Waters:	Yes, that comes to about £420, as I thought.
Ms March:	Oh no, it's that computer again. Those things are hardly worth the trouble, you know.
Mr Waters:	That's right. But they're wonderful as an excuse. Would you send us a cheque for the balance, then?
Ms March:	Yes, of course. I'll send you a cheque at once. Awfully sorry about this, Mr Waters. I'll put it in the mail today. Thanks for letting us know the mistake. Goodbye.
Mr Waters:	OK. Bye bye.

STUDENT 'A' ROLE PLAYS (TASK 13)

Unit 1

A1 Your name is Lesley Acheson from Sydney, Australia. You met Mr O'Brien from Supermotors Inc. in Australia and said you would call him. Ring Supermotors and ask to speak to him.

A2 You are Reginald Johnson, Autoparts Ltd. Ring Sarah Williams at Supermotors Inc. You would like to have your order (AC67745M) one week earlier than agreed.

A3 You are interested in importing fresh pineapples from the Philippines. Contact their Fruit Export Council agent in London and find the name and address of the best person to contact.

Unit 2

A1 You are William Tegetmeier, Megadecorations Inc. Call Susan Chan in Hong Kong. You would like her to confirm that she can meet you at 10 a.m. on Monday 14 May in your office.

A2 Try the same call again.

A3 You are Philip Brown. You have an interesting business idea that you want to discuss with Bruno Lampard (a friend of yours gave you his name). Ring him to arrange a meeting as early as possible next week. You'd like to take him out for lunch and then talk for an hour or so.

Unit 3

A1 You are Selena Jones, a buyer for the Southern Philadelphia Furniture Centre. Ring Supersit Inc. You would like to buy 450 model A1 Supersit kitchen chairs. Get the best discount you can. Don't accept less than 10%. You have bought 600 A1 chairs over the last two years.

A2 Ring Global Travel and book a flight from London to Torino. You can decide on the date when you want to travel. You want the cheapest possible flight and you'd like to arrive in time for lunch. Your name is Eastholm.

A3 You are a salesman for Compsell in London. Ring Jane Lever and give her a price on the Datapower 512 computer – £1650. This is relatively expensive but it includes installation, a two-year guarantee, service for three years and half a day's training. Computer shops, which are cheaper than your company, normally offer installation and a six month guarantee but no service or training. Come down to £1500 if necessary.

Unit 4

A1 You are meeting some important guests and would like to take them out to dinner. Ring the Grand Palace Restaurant and book a table for four people at 8 p.m. today.

A2 Make a call to the restaurant that has been recommended to you.

A3 Use your own name. You need a hotel room in Bergen, Norway, for five nights from 17 January. Your company pays you NOK (Norwegian Crowns) 1250 per day for hotel accommodation. If the difference in price is not too great, you'd like your wife/husband to accompany you. Ring the Sola Beach Hotel. A friend has recommended it.

Unit 5

You are on holiday in Britain and would like to hire a car. You'd like a small car for the weekend. Phone Rentacar Ltd (A1) and then Cheaprent Ltd (A2) and see what they can offer you. The total cost (without petrol) must be under £30.

A3 You hold a ticket on flight BA 312 from London to Paris at 18.00 on Friday 19 September. You know you will be a little delayed. Change your booking to the Air France flight (AF 794) that leaves one hour later.

Unit 6

A1 Your name is Sara Leijonflycht. You work for the Data Communications division of Scandata AB. You will be in London in week 48 and would very much like to meet Derek Hodgson, British Telecom's Euronet manager, to discuss using some of your company's equipment. You are free on Monday morning and from Wednesday lunchtime to the end of the week. From Monday lunchtime until Wednesday lunchtime you are with BCL Computers outside London. Phone Derek Hodgson.

A2 You are Peter Probe, Chairman of the Scottish Association of Market Researchers. Ring Professor Patricia Malcolm and see if she is prepared to be the keynote speaker at your next conference (opening day 16 November). You can offer her a fee of £275. The theme of the conference is 'Recent developments in market research'.

Unit 7

A1 You are staying at the Bristol Hotel. You ordered, by telephoning Room Service, continental breakfast (with tea) and the London *Times*. You have received continental breakfast (with coffee) and the *New York Times*. Ring Room Service, ask for the manager and complain.

A2 You asked Brown Trading Ltd for information about their F12 photocopier. They have sent you information about the F13. The information is in German and not, as you requested, in English. Ring and complain.

A3 Your name is Kiyoaki Arai. You booked a flight from Hong Kong to Tokyo from the hotel (the Meridien) by ringing Kowloon Travel Services. The ticket has now been delivered. The date and time of day are correct, but you specifically asked for Business Class on Cathay Pacific and they have booked you on JAL discount economy. Ring and complain.

Unit 8

A1 You are visiting the USA. You have a letter that you'd like to send to Greece, insured if possible. It weighs about 20 grammes. Ring a post office and get the necessary information.

A2 You have a booking on Air Florida flight FA 806 from Miami to New York. It arrives at Kennedy International at 19.15 but you need to be there at 19.00 at the latest in order to transfer to your flight back to Switzerland. Ring a travel agency and change your booking.

A3 You are José Ordonez. You have an appointment with Joanne Spencer in New York at 10 a.m. on Tuesday 17 May. It is now 9 a.m. on Tuesday and you are in Philadelphia. Your flight was diverted there because of fog over New York. Ring Ms Spencer, apologise and see if you can postpone your meeting for 24 hours.

KEY

▷**M**◁ = model answer (other correct answers are possible)

UNIT 1

Task 1

1 278 0040/Singapore/in a meeting
2 515 56 24/Saudi Arabia/at a conference

Task 2   ▷**M**◁

1 Georg Wenzel called. Call him on 010 49 40 80 70 55.
2 Ahmed Mansour called. He's flying back to Saudi Arabia tomorrow but will call you tonight.

Task 3

1 calling   2 moment   3 see   4 hold the line   5 ring up   6 in   7 reach, after
8 back

Task 4

1 b   2 a   3 a   4 b   5 b   6 c

Task 5

1 Ron Benson/Tom Parker/Maria Edwardes' address/Ron Benson
2 Mr Datta/Chris Ingersoll/putting order forward/Mr Datta

Task 6   ▷**M**◁

1 She's got an import/export office.
2 He's going to look it up.

3 It's MU/3721.
4 Two KS pump motors and a series of spare parts.
5 In April.

Task 7 ▷M◁

1 From: Ron Benson
   To: Tom Parker
   Information: Miss Maria Edwardes, 18 Dones Street, Cavite City, Manila.
2 From: Mr Datta
   To: Chris Ingersoll
   Information: Whole order available by 20 April
                Garston Motors will telex new arrangements

Task 8

1 e 2 g 3 b 4 n 5 m 6 k 7 c 8 f 9 h 10 a 11 l 12 j 13 i
14 d

Task 9

1 Could you tell me who you want to speak to, please?
2 Can you give me your telephone number, please?
3 Could you spell your name, please?
4 Would you repeat your address, please?
5 Can you tell me when you will be in the office tomorrow, please?
6 Would you confirm the delivery date, please?

Task 10

1 Chinese 2 America 3 Jordan 4 French 5 Germany 6 Japanese
7 Spanish 8 Dutch 9 Switzerland 10 Brazilian 11 Malaysia 12 Swedish
13 Egyptian 14 Belgium 15 Mexican 16 Irish

Task 12 ▷M◁

1 a No, I'm afraid it isn't. Bob's in a meeting right now. Can I take a message?
  b She's at the warehouse at the moment. Would you like to ring back later?
  c She's working at home this morning. You can call her on 85471.
  d I'm afraid Bob's gone home. I can give you his home number if it's urgent.
  e I'm sorry, Chris isn't here at the moment. She'll be back soon. Can I give her
     a message?
  f She's out of the office this afternoon, I'm afraid. Can I help you?

2 a Yes, can I speak to Mr Mayo, please?
  b OK, I'll ring you back if you like.
  c Hello, I'd like to speak to somebody about the price of your KS pump motors.
  d Would you ask her to ring me back when she comes in? She has the number.

Task 14

1 dial telephone   2 press-button telephone   3 directory   4 dial   5 handset
6 code   7 number   8 message pad

UNIT 2

Task 1

1 John Shackleton/Mrs Atkins/operator
2 Takiro Watanabe/John Williams/operator

Task 2

1 T   2 F   3 T   4 T

Task 3

1 dialled   2 extension   3 troubled   4 radiopager   5 directory   6 stand
7 checked   8 confirm   9 problems   10 appointment

Task 4

1 a   2 b   3 b   4 a   5 c   6 c

Task 5

1 Peter Wilson/Mr Hewitt, Packard Enterprises/Operator, Packard Electric/not known
2 Bob Troy/Jack Nelson/Jack Nelson/to arrange a meeting

Task 6

1 Mr Max/Pat Thompson/consignment of surfboards and sail material
2 Pat Thompson/Cathy Lester/delivery of 8 surfboards

Task 7   ▷M◁

1 He is a supplier of surfboards (and other sports equipment).
2 There are two containers. Both contain surfboards and one also contains nylon sail material.
3 Because he's too busy.
4 Buying surfboards and sails.
5 Because the instructor has to check the equipment.

Task 8

1 l   2 f   3 e   4 k   5 d   6 j   7 a   8 h   9 m   10 b   11 g   12 i   13 n   14 c

Task 9

1 When will Mr Drake be back?
2 Why hasn't the sales office called?
3 When does he normally arrive at the office?
4 Why has the consignment been delayed?
5 What do you/I dial for directory inquiries?
6 Where are you phoning from?
7 When could I reach him?
8 What does the number unobtainable tone sound like?

Task 10   ▷M◁

1 trnsprt   2 Jpn   3 rcmmnd   4 prsn   5 spk   6 driving exhibition next wk
7 consignment delayed 1 mth   8 book room 2 nghts   9 find map area?   10 when lamp lit, set up call

Task 12   ▷M◁

1 Sorry, I must have dialled the wrong number.
2 But he asked me to call today. Are you sure he isn't there?
3 This appointment we've been trying to arrange. Well, Monday would suit me.
4 I'm afraid this is the wrong extension. (Just a moment) I'll put you on/through to the switchboard.

Task 14   ▷M◁

1 Four.
2 No, it offers the widest service available.
3 Yes, regionally or locally as well as nationally.
4 Nothing. You dial 100 and ask for 'Freefone Radiopaging'.

UNIT 3

Task 1

1 Mr Murray/Mr Parker/buying shares
2 Ms Matsumoto/Globe Travel/flights to Penang

Task 2 ▷M◁

1 Mr Murray. About shares (Electroworks)
   Contact stocks department. Ring back in half an hour.
2 Ms Matsumoto. To Penang next week. Economy flight.
   Dep Friday 9 June. Malaysian Airlines excursion, HK$1950 return. Cathay Pacific HK$2160. Malaysian Airlines dep 9.40 arr 12.00. CP dep 11.40 arr 14.30.

Task 3

1 lowest 2 allow, quantity 3 gone up 4 demand 5 special 6 cost
7 repeat 8 Share

Task 4

1 c 2 a 3 a 4 b 5 c 6 b

Task 5 ▷M◁

1 BSO concert sold out, possibility of cancellations at box office, price $10
2 Ed Reilly, 2-year-old car to trade in, interested in new Cutlass Supreme, new model on display in showroom, will visit after work

Task 6

1 a Pat Thompson, Weald b Dugardin c tents d XT12 e PT20
f 610 francs g 774 francs
2 a Jim Hampton, Blacktons b Weald c footballs d £9.20 e 9%

Task 7 ▷M◁

1 100
2 Sample cuttings showing new colours
3 Super A quality
4 7% quantity discount, 2% cash discount
5 He'll put it in writing and mail it

Task 8

1 e 2 l 3 d 4 i 5 a 6 k 7 h 8 j 9 b 10 g 11 c 12 f

Task 9 ▷M◁

1 Sven Larsson said he was arriving on BA 651.
2 Mr Dutronc said he wants at least thirty in the first delivery.
3 The travel agency clerk said you could fly on MAS 1832.
4 Peter Novak said there's an extra 2% discount for cash.
5 The Sales Manager said he had received your order, Mrs Pertile.
6 Mr Jackson said that was the best price we could offer, Mr Blanchard.
7 The clerk said that your order has been dispatched, Mr Klein.
8 Mrs Reid said she'd wait for you at the restaurant, Mr Reid.

Task 10

1 NB 2 e.g. 3 p.a. 4 etc. 5 ETA 6 GMT 7 TLX 8 SAE 9 ASAP
10 CIF 11 fob 12 RE 13 max. 14 dep. 15 ATTN 16 esp. 17 Ask
Dittmar re invoice asap 18 CIF $27 000 19 18% p.a. interest 20 Agent ETA
London 22.30 21 NB changed dep. time

Task 12 ▷M◁

Yes, please. I'm planning to fly to Madrid. (Can I get an excursion ticket?)
....
On the 6th April.
....
(About) a week.
....
That's fine. Can you make the reservation for me, please?

Task 14

1 5 2 42.80 kr 3 00944 904 34561 4 58.50 kr
5 Malta, Turkey, France, Luxembourg, Canada, USA 6 7

UNIT 4

Task 1

1 Fast Taxi Service / Barbara Lee / ordering a taxi for Changi Airport
2 Reliance Company / Edward Bronson / ordering a bicycle
3 City Trading Company / — / placing an order

Key

Task 2

1 T 2 F 3 T 4 F 5 F 6 F

Task 3

1 place 2 note 3 quote, catalogue 4 rush 5 pay, account 6 bill
7 dispatch 8 freight 9 repeat 10 catch

Task 4

1 b 2 c 3 b 4 c 5 c 6 a

Task 5

1 Worldwide Flowers/Jim Kelly/43 Pennsylvania Ave, Bloomington, Indiana,
   47401/12 red roses/before 6 p.m. on September 12
2 Western Liquor Distribution/Bill Patterson/Patterson's Liquor in Albany/California
   (Nappa) red wine/by the end of the week

Task 6 ▷M◁

1 Weald 1000 XT 12 @ 560 francs, send to London Heathrow asap, cheque in mail
   today
2 McPhersons (Edinburgh) Champion tennis shoes, 50 pairs sizes 36–44, 30 pairs
   sizes 35 and 45, immediate delivery

Task 7 ▷M◁

1 50 francs on each tent
2 By draft on Dugardin's bank or by cheque
3 There has been a rush on tennis shoes
4 Not enough are obtainable in all the sizes needed
5 At the beginning of August

Task 8

1 f 2 b 3 g 4 c 5 j 6 a 7 e 8 i 9 k 10 h 11 d

Task 9

1 arrives 2 are visiting 3 opens 4 starts 5 are going 6 are meeting

Task 10

1 delivery 2 information 3 cost 4 inquiry 5 charge 6 confirmation
7 call 8 suggest 9 reservation 10 book 11 cancel 12 quote
13 arrangement 14 translate 15 page 16 flight

Task 12 ▷M◁

Yes, I'd like to place an order for the tent I've seen in your catalogue.

....
XD 4986.

....
No, wait a moment. It's XD 4986.

....
Yes, it's . . . (name and address of student).

....
(Student spells name).

....
Thank you. Goodbye.

Task 14

1 Four: three keys and a slide switch.
2 Yes, a volume control on the side.
3 Press the 'Store' key.
4 Move the slide switch to the right.

UNIT 5

Task 1

1 Aston Tours and Travel/Spain/a Marbella   b Torremolinos
2 Globe Travel/Malaysia (Penang)/a Malaysian Airlines   b Cathay Pacific

Task 2

1 T 2 T 3 F 4 F 5 F

Task 3

1 double   2 departure   3 airlines, convenient   4 scheduled   5 check-in
6 apartment   7 facilities   8 kept   9 arrangements, hearing   10 locally, prefer

Task 4

1 a   2 c   3 b   4 b   5 a   6 c

Task 5

1 Elaine Morrison/Boston/Ritz Carlton/26 and 27 July/single with bath
2 The university/———/Excelsior/14–20 September/double

Task 6

1 29 March   2 10 April   3 dinner   4 Watford   5 9 and 10 April   6 phone
number   7 King's Head Hotel   8 station   9 0923 7372218   10 10.45 a.m.

Task 7   ▷M◁

1 He couldn't find the customer he wanted to visit and they are not in business any
  more.
2 They will not get the money owed to them by the Evanson Company because it
  is bankrupt.
3 Newton and Welshpool.
4 Because he will have some news for him after the meeting on Thursday morning.

Task 8

1 f   2 b   3 g   4 j   5 a   6 k   7 d   8 l   9 i   10 c   11 h   12 e

Task 9

1 We might visit Sao Paulo on the way home.
2 The goods should reach you by the end of the week.
3 You should get a good discount from the car company.
4 The discount will be bigger if you order over 1000 units.
5 The reference number should be at the top of the page.
6 He will ring you before 12 tomorrow.

Task 10

1 They wanted to know if the order was firm.
2 He asked me what the reference number was.
3 He inquired if there was a bigger discount for larger orders.
4 She asked me where I had filed the records.
5 He wondered when the goods would reach them.
6 He asked me if we expected to receive the goods soon.
7 She asked me how long she had to wait.
8 She wanted to know whether I had booked my flight yet.
9 She wondered if she could pay by credit card.
10 He wanted to know where the goods would be delivered.

Task 12 ▷M◁

Hello, Weald here. We have a reservation for the 9th and 10th April and now I'm afraid I shall have to cancel it.

....

Mr Bengtsson.

....

No, I shall have to cancel it, I'm afraid.

....

Thank you, goodbye.

Task 14

1 F 2 F 3 T 4 F 5 T

UNIT 6

Task 1

1 Bob Ross/Andrew Brickwood/Friday/Argentinian visitor with change of itinerary/ Tuesday 12th June, 11.30
2 Ann Perkins/Mr Masterton/tomorrow (board meeting)/illness (influenza)/Martin Close to go to meeting instead

Task 2

1 F 2 T 3 F 4 T 5 T 6 F

Key

Task 3

1 recognise, away 2 itinerary, appointments 3 diary 4 tied up 5 attend
6 objectives, describe, services 7 delegate 8 smoothly 9 loudspeakers
10 checklist

Task 4

1 a 2 a 3 b 4 c 5 b 6 b

Task 5

1 John Deluca/Susan Johnson/problems with IBM-X20/Wednesday 2 p.m.
2 Cheryl Nelson/Frank Sharp/reply to job vacancy advert/Tuesday 9 a.m.

Task 6 ▷M◁

1 Pat Thompson phoned. Weald's conference next month for agents and a few influen-
tial customers. About 150. Probably Northwest Conference Hall. Lunch with Pat
next Wednesday. I must confirm by phone.
2 Weald, manufacturers/wholesalers of sports equipment. Heard me at symposium
on advertising one year ago. Want 50-minute talk on cost-effective publicity 21
Sept a.m. Small groups/workshops after talk. £200 plus expenses.

Task 7 ▷M◁

1 Because she made most of the arrangements for the previous one.
2 To introduce next season's products, describe services to customers and so on.
3 It's expensive.
4 Because he's not very interested in sport.
5 Because he's a well-known authority on his subject.

Task 8

1 e 2 a 3 j 4 g 5 f 6 h 7 b 8 d 9 i 10 c

Task 9

1 If Weald's products were not well advertised, their sales would fall.
2 We would consider using another supplier if our supplier stopped our discount.
3 If the speaker couldn't come to the conference, we would look for a replacement.
4 I would book on another airline if the TWA flight was cancelled.

5 There would be a drop in revenue if our market share decreased suddenly.
6 If the value of the pound fell, Weald's exports would be more competitively priced.

Task 10 ▷M◁

 1 A reference number.
 2 A tone that informs you that the number is unobtainable.
 3 York area code.
 4 A call connect system.
 5 A system for communicating text electronically.
 6 Subscriber trunk dialling.
 7 An orchestra from Boston that plays symphonies.
 8 Codes with three digits for countries.
 9 An airline seat reservation system.
10 A call lasting six minutes made at lunch time on Monday.

Task 12 ▷M◁

(Student's name)
....
Sorry, I'm afraid I'm tied up at 12.00.
....
I'll just check. I'm free at 3.00.

Task 14 ▷M◁

1 No, not 1p.
2 The display flashes and you hear the paytone (rapid pips).
3 Press the blue follow-on call button, then continue as before.
4 Two: SOS emergency calls and calls to the operator.

UNIT 7

Task 1 ▷M◁

1 To: Mr MacDougall. From: Mr Janssen, Janssen Co., Hilversum, Holland, tel: 3135
   789280. Mr MacDougall to call back asap (before 12 our time).
2 Janssen, Janssen Co., Hilversum. 600 cases of Whitehill Malt stuck at the customs.
   Incomplete details. Contact forwarding agents. Ring Janssen Co. today. Leave message after 12 our time.

Task 2

1 T   2 F   3 F   4 T   5 F   6 F

Task 3

1 serious, urgent 2 consignment 3 delayed 4 forwarding agents 5 processes
6 wrong 7 mix-up 8 sorry, inconvenience

Task 4

1 b 2 c 3 a 4 c 5 b 6 a

Task 5

1 Doug Saxton/Mrs Sullivan/Sun Air/incorrect information about flight schedules
2 Jim Adams/Sam Jacobs/Brand Names Mail Order/wrong tape recorder model sent

Task 6 ▷M◁

1 Tomlin Order no.: 0073921. Order mix-up – one box OK, two boxes wrong. Find out reason and call back at 2.30.
2 Order no.: 0073921. Tomlin Sport, Warrington. One box OK, two incorrectly labelled (should have been sent to Warringtons Stores, Birmingham). Send two boxes ex-stock to Tomlin. Jim Graham will bring new job card. Ask Tomlin to redirect the two boxes.

Task 7 ▷M◁

1 He's received the wrong tennis shoes.
2 The order processing department.
3 By referring to the order number.
4 By asking someone in the warehouse.
5 He'll ring Mr Tomlin back and let him know the position.
6 When he knows the order number, he checks it with the delivery note.
7 Two boxes were not correctly labelled. They went to Tomlin Sport instead of Warringtons Stores, Birmingham.
8 To send Tomlin Sport the right shoes from stock and ask them to redirect the wrong ones to Birmingham.
9 The necessary job card from Mr Graham.
10 The same day.

Task 8

1 f 2 b 3 g 4 j 5 a 6 d 7 i 8 c 9 h 10 e

Task 9

1 I'm sorry. We should have labelled them correctly.
2 I'm sorry. We should have told you about that.
3 I'm sorry. We should have checked your order.
4 I'm sorry. We should have given you more exact information.
5 I'm sorry. We should have reserved a table (for you).
6 I'm sorry. We should have put one in the box.

Task 10

1 I'll have it checked.
2 I'll have it fixed.
3 I'll have them forwarded.
4 I'll have it sent.
5 I'll have them dispatched at once.
6 I'll have them brought down.

Task 12   ▷M◁

It's Johnson Brothers here. I'm afraid I have to make a complaint.

....

The invoice you sent us isn't correct.

....

The invoice number is 6597 and our order number is 4102.

....

You've invoiced us for 30 clips, but we only ordered 13.

Task 14   ▷M◁

1 When there are a number of participants in different locations.
2 When there are a number of participants at the same location.
3 To avoid travel expenses and travelling time.
4 Because the participants need to travel to the conference TV studio.
5 $40.
6 It is not likely that there will be a conference TV studio in the town.

UNIT 8

Task 1

1 Reliance Mail Order Company / Mr Bronson / overdue payment / Mr Bronson to contact bank / from Mr Bronson or his bank
2 Carlos Rodríguez / Flyway Airlines / missing luggage / Flyway Airlines to trace luggage / Flyway to contact Mr Rodríguez

Key

Task 2

1 F   2 T   3 T   4 T   5 F

Task 3

1 overdue   2 details/information, sort   3 nuisance   4 something,
details/information   5 form, declaration   6 baggage   7 reached   8 leave

Task 4

1 c   2 c   3 b   4 a   5 c   6 c

Task 5

1 Fred Barnes/Bargain Rental/a misunderstanding about a discount/the company
  will return the mileage charge
2 Ron Smith/Mike's Sporting Goods/a request for a contribution to help young ath-
  letes/$100 will be contributed

Task 6

1 Herr Lang/7 tents are useless/send photos of the damage/send replacements asap
2 Christine March/insufficient compensation/none/send cheque for the balance

Task 7   ▷M◁

1 Investigate the matter if he gets a fuller description of the damage.
2 He will have the tents photographed and send the photos to Herr Lang.
3 He will send replacement tents as soon as he can.
4 He apologises on behalf of the company and thanks Mr Kumar for his help.
5 He wants Mr Kumar to keep them in the meantime.
6 £420 and £369.60.
7 A computer error.
8 A cheque for the balance.

Task 8

1 d   2 e   3 g   4 i   5 h   6 c   7 f   8 b   9 j   10 a

Task 9

1 may/could/might   2 may/could/might   3 should/ought to   4 can't   5 must
6 must   7 should/ought to   8 may/could/might

Task 10

1 announcement   2 schedule   3 lunch   4 apology   5 preference   6 state
7 complaint   8 reference   9 describe   10 prepare   11 delay   12 arrive
13 recommendation   14 please   15 transmit   16 departure

Task 12   ▷M◁

1 What was your order number, please?
   ....
   Ah yes, 3216. Something has obviously gone wrong. I'll have the order checked.
2 I'm sorry. There does seem to have been a mistake at our end. Thanks for telling
   me about it.
3 Yes, sir. Can we come and give you a demonstration?

Task 14

1 d   2 e   3 b   4 j   5 i   6 h   7 g   8 a   9 c   10 f

APPENDIX: INTERNATIONAL TELEPHONE ALPHABETS

These telephone alphabets are used to spell names, addresses and other words, and are easier to hear and distinguish than the letters alone.

ICAO PHONETIC ALPHABET
(International Civil Aviation Organisation)

Aviation and Radio

A – Alfa	H – Hotel	O – Oscar	V – Victor
B – Bravo	I – India	P – Papa	W – Whisky
C – Charlie	J – Juliet	Q – Quebec	X – X-ray
D – Delta	K – Kilo	R – Romeo	Y – Yankee
E – Echo	L – Lima	S – Sierra	Z – Zulu
F – Foxtrot	M – Mike	T – Tango	
G – Golf	N – November	U – Uniform	

BRITISH TELEPHONE ALPHABET

A – Alfred	H – Harry	O – Oliver	V – Victor
B – Benjamin	I – Isaac	P – Peter	W – William
C – Charles	J – Jack	Q – Queen	X – X-ray
D – David	K – King	R – Robert	Y – Yellow
E – Edward	L – London	S – Samuel	Z – Zebra
F – Frederick	M – Mary	T – Tommy	
G – George	N – Nellie	U – Uncle	

THE INTERNATIONAL SPELLING ANALOGY

A – Amsterdam	H – Havana	O – Oslo	V – Valencia
B – Baltimore	I – Italy	P – Paris	W – Washington
C – Casablanca	J – Jerusalem	Q – Quebec	X – Xantippe
D – Denmark	K – Kilogram	R – Roma	Y – Yokohama
E – Edison	L – Liverpool	S – Santiago	Z – Zürich
F – Florida	M – Madagascar	T – Tripoli	
G – Gallipoli	N – New York	U – Upsala	

CAMBRIDGE PROFESSIONAL ENGLISH
A new range of flexible materials, designed to meet the needs of today's English learners in a business and professional environment.

Telephoning in English

Telephoning in English is for professionals or trainee professionals in a wide range of fields in business, commerce and administration who need to make and answer telephone calls in English. It is suitable for learners at intermediate and upper-intermediate levels.

The emphasis is on developing and consolidating *practical* telephone skills in a variety of interesting and relevant contexts. Activities range from message-taking and spelling practice to role-play, providing learners with a comprehensive course in using the telephone in English.

★ Covers a range of common telephone situations

★ Relevant and up-to-date contexts

★ Contains lively and communicative activities

★ For use in class, or for self-study

★ Can be used on its own, or in combination with other material

★ Intermediate level

★ Widely tested before publication

★ Authors highly experienced in English for Specific Purposes

Cover design by Ken Vail

ISBN 0-521-26975-X

9 780521 269759